Getting the Best Start in Therapy

A consumer guide to beginning counselling and psychotherapy

A therapist guide to client concerns beginning therapy

EmpoweringYourTherapy.com

Edition 1.03

Mamood Ahmad

© 2020

Also by the same Author:

Success in Therapy

Subscribe to Dear Therapist **(on YouTube)**
for weekly videos about mental health and therapy

Twitter: @ahmad_mamood

Table of Contents

Dedicated to all worldwide consumers of therapy and particularly those clients who have been failed by bad therapy. This book was written because of you. Your voice and struggle have not been forgotten.

Therapy is truth, your truth

Introduction

Therapy, sometimes called counselling or psychotherapy, can and does change lives. Overwhelming evidence confirms the successful use of therapy for what appears to be an inexhaustible list of psychological problems, such as depression, anxiety, stress, trauma and abuse. As well as particular problems, therapy for many is an opportunity for them to be the best version of themselves, and to gain self-knowledge, insight and growth. Through self-understanding, people often find improvements in relationships and work, and they find increased happiness, meaning and joy in their lives. However, it can be a daunting prospect, especially if you haven't worked with a therapist before or don't know if therapy (or the therapist) is going to suitable for you.

This book aims to empower your beginning in therapy by helping you feel confident about therapy, how and why therapy works, what problems it can help with, finding the right therapist, navigating the multitude of options and approaches, as well as answering your questions and concerns. You'll learn about what to expect at the initial session and understand contracting considerations.

For therapists and trainee therapists, many parts of this book will be familiar. However, the material here is an accumulation of knowledge, based on my research and experience of clients, about their questions and concerns as they begin therapy. These concerns are addressed throughout this book, and I hope they will be provide a source for reflection and client-centred adaptation in attuning to what consumers may need from us. In addition, I have created an Inventory of Concerns questionnaire (Appendix D) you may wish to consider using with your clients to elicit these concerns. By working with clients on concerns there is potential to activate client empowerment, align expectations, identify constraints, correct misinformation, identify process interference, tune in your approach, build the relationship, and of course, content for the process.

Here are some of the biggest questions addressed in this book, if you are entering therapy you may well be asking some of these questions:

- What is therapy? What is it like? How can this possibly work? You may be confused about how or why therapy would work as it appears to be "just talking".

- Is therapy going to work for me? Is it really an option? How do I navigate the minefield of therapy approaches, options and therapists available? Am I making the right choices?

- How will I know I am working with a good therapist who is competent and will be able to help and keep me safe?

- What can I expect when beginning therapy? What can I do to prepare and what do I need to be aware of when contracting for therapy? What if the therapist does not want to work with me? What can I do to make the best of therapy? What is my role?

- Vulnerability or performance related questions. Am I going to be judged? And not understood or told I'm wrong? What if I don't perform well? What if I can't say what I need to say? What can I do if I find it hard to be vulnerable? What if I don't want to talk about something? How do I deal with the proximity intimacy of face to face setting and the embarrassment of going to therapy?

- Will I be safe? How confidential is confidential? What if I am part of a legal trial? Or I want to have records kept of what I talk about? Will I or someone I know get into trouble? What are my rights in therapy?

- How is therapy going to impact my life? Financially, time, effort, my wellbeing and relationships? How can I reduce the financial cost of going to therapy?

- How can I support someone who is in therapy? How can I get someone to access help when they don't want to?

- Does it matter that the therapist has recovered from similar problems to me? Or comes from the same cultural or similar beliefs system

- Does the therapist gender, age, and how much they charge matter? Should I work with a trainee? I keep finding the "wrong" therapist?

Although I cannot promise you by reading this book your beginnings in therapy will be plain sailing, I do hope you'll be empowered by this book. Let's face it, life's too short to waste on therapy that's unnecessarily inefficient or ineffective. Your happiness and wellbeing are important. Good luck on your therapeutic adventure.

Once you have begun therapy you may be interested in my follow up book, 21 Ways to Success in therapy, which is an in-depth, practical and accessible guide to navigating your therapeutic process in order to be successful within it.

If you have any feedback or questions related to this book, please contact me ma@paththerapy.co.uk or join my Youtube channel: "Dear therapist" where you'll find weekly videos from therapists on a wide range of mental health and therapy related matters

The book is structured into three parts. The following topics are covered by this book:

- Chapter 1 – Understanding therapy
    - What therapy is and what it is not
    - How and why therapy works
    - What problems therapy can be used for
    - How to spot early signs of emotional and mental health problems
- Chapter 2 – Getting started in therapy
    - Understand and assess therapy options including access methods, short and long term therapy, approaches, tools and the setting for therapy
    - Finding the right therapist for you including therapist standards, experience, questions to ask and relational considerations
    - Your rights in therapy
    - Understand risks associated with disclosure of information during therapy
    - How to get the most out of therapy
    - What to expect at your first session including preparedness
    - Why a therapist may not be able to work with you
    - What you may need to consider when contracting with a therapist
- Chapter 3 – Client Matters: Beginning therapy. Addresses others concerns you may have prior to beginning therapy.
- Appendix A – Survey of common client concerns when beginning therapy
- Appendix B – Mental Health Support numbers
- Appendix C – Further support for consumers in therapy
- Appendix D – Eliciting your concerns

Who is this book for?

This books if for anyone interested in, considering or beginning their therapeutic process. If you have specific concerns you wish to understand I suggest reading the table of contents or the next section "Your concerns answered" to quickly find the information you are looking for.

If you are a therapist, therapist trainer, supervisor or trainee therapist you could utilise this resource, either for your own clients or to review how you engage in your beginnings with clients, thus contributing to better outcomes in the early stages of the process. Knowing the wide variety of client concerns can enhance your understanding of client process

Your concerns answered

I have been collecting information from clients about what concerns them most before they enter therapy. Overall there are three categories of concerns that people have before they enter therapy. First, suitability concerns about whether therapy will work and the fit with the therapist will be right. Second, whether they will be able to fulfil their role in therapy to do what is needed. Third, the impact therapy will have on their lives. The tables below show these list of concerns per category and where those concerns are addresses in this book.

If you are interested, I have collected statistics in Appendix A which shows the most common concerns that clients have. Understanding that any concerns you have are normal can help alleviate any worries you may have.

The table below lists **suitability concerns** about therapy, the therapist and the setting of therapy.

Description	Book Section
Whether the therapist is competent	Finding the right therapist -> Therapist Standards
Whether the therapist is right for me	Finding the right therapist -> Therapist Experience & Relational Considerations
Whether therapy will work for me	The First Session
Whether I have chosen the right type of therapy (E.g. CBT, Person Centred)	Assessing Therapy Options -> Approaches to Therapy
Whether therapy is a suitable option for my problems	What problems can therapy be used for?
The therapist judging you or saying you are wrong	What is therapy -> What therapy is not
Being alone in a room with the therapist. Worried about the intimacy of the setting. Emotional disclosure and being face to face.	The First Session-> Informing of Significant Needs & Client Matters -> Encounter concerns

Description	Book Section
The therapist will be able to understand my ethnicity (your cultural or national tradition)	Client matters -> Identification Matters
The therapist will not understand me (in general)	Client matters -> Not being understood
Whether I will have to talk about something I don't want to	What is therapy -> What therapy is not
Whether the location is suitable	The First Session -> Informing of significant needs

The table below lists **performance or role concerns** about client's ability to make use of therapy, their role, and fears about therapy.

Description	Book Section
Being able to perform well enough in therapy. Trusting yourself to use the sessions well, to know how to use and get the most out of them. Knowing what to talk about and doing therapy right. I will freeze up and not be able to talk.	Client Matters -> Am I doing this right & How to get the most out of therapy
Talking about your problems and what has happened. The content of therapy.	Client Matters -> Am I doing this right
I will get triggered emotionally or physically. (You feel that your existing emotional or physical symptoms will be exacerbated by attending therapy. For example, flashback, a phobic reaction, panic, emotional state, fainting, anxiety)	The First Session -> Informing of significant needs, Finding the right therapist -> Relational considerations, Client Matters -> Keeping safe in therapy
Fear of feeling vulnerable. I will get upset in front of the therapist.	Client Matters -> Challenge of the encounter

The table below lists **life impacting concerns** about the consequences of change, the commitment, wellbeing, and disclosure.

Description	Book Section
I am worried about the financial commitment	Client Matters -> Therapy on a budget, Assessing Therapy options
I am worried about the time and commitment needed	Assessing Therapy Options, Client Matters -> Money and Time
I will change and it would have consequences for me and others	Client Matters -> Life Impacts
I will feel worse by going to therapy	Client Matters -> Life Impacts
I will find out something about myself I don't like	Client Matters -> Life Impacts
The stigma of being in therapy or seeing a therapist	Client Matters -> Stigma
Someone will find out you are in therapy e.g. someone your know sees you	Client Matters -> Stigma
I or someone close to me going to get in trouble if I disclose something to the therapist	Disclosure

Important bits

You can ready through sections or dip in and out of the topics covered that you feel are relevant to you. Some topics may relate to more in which case you can take more time to understand, absorb and reflect while using the self-help reflection questions.

✓ You're going to take these ideas and reflect on whether they fit you. As with all important matters in life, you are a free and autonomous human being, so you are free to choose what is useful and what isn't. If you're unsure, you may of course talk to your therapist; in fact, it's highly recommended.

✓ This book is based on generic therapy processes and is agnostic to any type (or *modality*) of therapy. It has been reviewed by a number of UK qualified therapists across the spectrum: psychodynamic, person-centred, existential and CBT. This does not mean that all therapists will agree completely with the material presented. Therefore, it is highly recommend you talk about things that come from this book with your therapist.

✓ The book assumes you are working with a good-enough therapist—one who can accept all your feelings and work with them with empathy and non-judgement. However, just like all professions, there is no guarantee how well informed or sensitive the therapist is.

✓ Please bear in mind that therapists can challenge your behaviors and also share opinions, but they should do so sensitively, openly and in a way that is aligned to your interests and therapeutic goals.

✓ This book is not a replacement for therapy or a therapist. The intention is to empower your therapy process and strengthen the work you are doing, not interfere with it.

✓ This book is written for international consumers of therapy. However, since each country may have its own variations e.g. competence standards, I have written for a UK audience and indicated where **international variations** may exist depending on your country.

Further Support

If you need more external help with your therapy process, you can contact your country's regulatory, governing body or voluntary membership body (See Appendix B for main UK bodies). See Appendix C for other additional coaching support for people in therapy.

Chapter 1: Understanding Therapy

This chapter aims to give you a good understanding of what therapy is, what therapy can help with, and how and why it works.

What is therapy?

Therapy, also called psychotherapy or counselling, is an activity by which you meet with a therapist to work on problems in your life. These problems can be wide ranging from relationships, behaviors, life decisions, traumatic experiences, bereavement as well as bodily symptoms such as panic. Therapy may also be used by people seeking self-improvement and growth unaccompanied by any specific problem, because you just want to be the best version of yourself, whether it's seeking life purpose or seeking to understand yourself better. Ultimately, beginning therapy can be a big step toward being the healthiest version of yourself and living the best life possible.

This activity of therapy is primarily based on talking to explore thoughts and feelings in relationship with the therapist who is skilled, through training and experience, in helping people resolve these types of problems. The activity of therapy is held within a relational space, where you, your problems and any content that comes up is accepted with empathy. Therapy does not offer medication or diagnose mental health issues, although those may be sought alongside therapy through a psychiatrist and/or a psychologist. The therapist may use a variety of tools or techniques based on their own training and skills to help you during the process. There are a number of types (called modalities) of therapies which therapist have trained in. Popular therapies include Cognitive Behavioral Therapy (CBT), Person Centered, Psychodynamic, or Integrative therapy. Although these modalities differ in theoretical approach, or what they believe helps clients change, they all universally agree that the relationship between the client and therapist is the foundation for good therapy regardless of the modality they practice. Therapy may be provided either individually, between you and a therapist, or as a couple, group or family, called individual, couples, group and family therapy respectively.

International Variation: In some countries the term counselling can refer to support, coaching, listening and advice giving, rather than therapy. If you're unsure whether you're receiving therapy you should talk to the provider. A suggestion could be to ask whether they are using a particular modality as the basis for counselling. Samaritans UK is one example of a listening service rather than a counselling one.

What therapy is not
If you're deciding whether therapy is going to be a good choice for you, you can also take a look at the things therapy is not.

Therapy is not about judging you

Therapy is not about telling you you're bad in some way or forcing you to do or talk about things you don't want to or telling you that you need to do better in therapy. Therapy is an open invitation for you to be yourself as you are, not as you may believe the therapist expects you to be. Therapy is about providing an accepting, empathic and safe environment for you to work on what you want to. If you feel nervous about sharing something that you are embarrassed about, those feelings are accepted too and it is quite normal; you can go at your own pace, when and if you're ready. Similarly, if you feel you're not "performing well" in therapy, therapists generally welcome that and are really accepting of it, even with big silences or with your anxiety in the room. They want you to feel you can be yourself.

Therapy is not just turning up

Therapy will only work if you actively do the work. If you're reluctant to be in therapy or you have expectations that turning up will be enough then its unlikely therapy will be successful. You will have to take part actively to stretch those mind and thought muscles. While physical exercise requires dedication, so too does therapy. Therapy is emotional training for wellbeing.

Therapy is not a magic pill to life's problems

Although a single session can be enough to help you, therapy is an opportunity to explore, gain better understanding and insights. You don't usually get fixed by just talking to someone, it's more reasonable to say the skilled therapist creates an environment by which healing can occur. You will have to put in the work, while the therapist is trained to provide the necessary conditions for you to do that collaboratively. You'll have to be prepared to put in the required time and effort to work towards creating inner emotional improvements.

Therapy is not advice giving

Therapists don't give advice about decisions in life. For example, don't expect the therapist to advise you on whether you're better off leaving a relationship, or whether to confront your parents about an issue, what they will do, through their expertise, is to help you to work out answers to your own questions. Only you can possibly make these decisions, you know you better, what you need and what works.

Having said that therapists, may give possible interpretations on what and why some of the things you're working are occurring, such as the impact of your childhood on the way you think and feel now. They may also advise on other services that may be able to support you outside of the service they provide, such as addiction support groups, mental health crisis lines or other supporting treatment options.

Therapy is not providing a friend who will listen

Therapy is based on a relationship called the therapist and client relationship, it is its own type of boundaried relationship alongside others we have in life such as friend, father or mother. While friends can offer support, therapy is based on solid theory and the experience of the therapist to help you overcome psychological difficulties. It is not a friendship because to be friends it would need to be reciprocal, but it provides a space where you don't have to worry about a friend's opinion and are free to set the agenda. It is its own relationship and it can even be deep and caring but it exists within boundaries to help you get the most out of therapy.

Therapy is not an emergency line

If you're in sudden crisis or emergency involving mental health, therapy is not generally for emergency access to help. As part of the therapy contract your therapist will make clear the service they provide and the boundaries of it. The therapist may signpost to out of hours support and emergency services. If you are concerned about getting help outside therapy it is recommended you raise this with your therapist.

Therapy is not at core about diagnosis

Some people may have or want a mental health diagnosis. Examples include autism, bipolar disorder, borderline personality disorder or post-traumatic stress disorder. In therapy, the diagnosis can help the therapist gain an initial understanding and even inform the way they provide therapy, but therapy sees that very much as a starting point and seeks to look behind the label to the whole person. Therapy is more about understanding the whole of you – the inner you, your story, feelings, what has shaped you and how that relates to any problems you share. In therapy, the therapist will be recognising you as more than any diagnosis or symptom; they will see you as a whole, unique and complex being. This does not mean therapists are against treating mental health issues with medication or don't believe in diagnoses; it just means they are trained to help with these issues by working within the context of your whole being, informed but not blinded by any diagnosis you may have.

Comparison with other psychological professionals

In this book I use the term therapist as an umbrella term for anyone who practices counselling or psychotherapy. Therapists are trained to work with you over short or long term to help to bring about psychological change and enhance wellbeing. They do so primarily by talking with you, though other tools, such as art or mindfulness may be used. Therapists don't typically diagnose you, and work with you within your mental world. They do not prescribe medication.

Therapists, in terms of counselling and psychotherapy, can often be confused with other types of wellbeing and mental health professionals and there are definitely overlaps, because ultimately they deal with mental improvement. Here are other types of professionals and the main differences in comparison to therapists.

- A Coach looks to identify and make changes a person needs and wants and what is holding them back from achieving it. Coaching looks at the issue, in the "here and now" and changes needed both internally and in the world to obtain confidence needed to achieve these goals. It's not typically associated with creating deep awareness of the past and how it impacts the present.
- Clinical Psychologist. Psychology is the scientific study of the mind in the way people behave, interact or think, both consciously and unconsciously. Psychologist may be skilled in diagnosis, for example a personality disorder.
- Psychiatrist. A psychiatrist is someone who has had medical training and has decided to specialise in psychiatry. The term psychiatry refers to the study of mental disorders. This includes their diagnosis, medication,

management and prevention. Psychiatrists often work on a broad range of cases alongside an area of expertise and research.

- Mediation. Mediators often work in workplaces, human resources and independently. They work to resolve differences between people. For example, difficulties with an ex-partner, or a work colleague.

Keyword: Here and now refers to what challenges and issues you are experiencing currently in your day to day existence rather than focusing on the past. The past may come up but the focus is on the now.

International Variation: Different countries may use different professional names or same names that mean something different

What problems can therapy be used for?

Therapy can be useful for many psychological problems. Therapy can be used for complex and severely distressing problems such as suffering from a psychosis where you hallucinate or hear voices, to life stresses such as feeling low due to work stress. In most cases, problems will be comorbid, where a number of problems coexist. Here are a brief description of the major categories of problems that people come to therapy for. This list is not exhaustive but indicative.

Life Stresses

Although a degree of stress is a healthy part of life, stress can build up incrementally and cause a variety of issues and symptoms such as difficulty sleeping or a general sense of feeling tired and run down. Specific stresses in life may include bereavement, relationship breakup, life-changing illness, work difficulties, financial difficulties, family troubles, or children not leaving home. Stress does not have to be related to negative experience, positive events can be stressful too, and such as moving house or getting married.

Anxiety

People with anxiety respond to certain objects or situations with fear and dread, as well as with physical signs of anxiety or panic, such as a rapid heartbeat and sweating. Fears could range from health anxiety, phobias e.g. fear of spiders, social anxiety to a general feeling of anxiety which may be continuously experienced.

A particular anxiety called OCD (Obsessive Compulsive Disorder) is where people have constant thoughts or fears that cause them to perform certain rituals or routines. The disturbing thoughts are called obsessions, and the rituals are called compulsions that try to cancel out those obsessions. An example is a person with an unreasonable fear of germs who constantly washes his or her hands.

Mood Issues

With mood related issues you may have persistent feelings of sadness, or fluctuations from extreme happiness to extreme sadness. Your moods may combine with other emotions such as anger, emptiness, numbness or tearfulness. The most common mood issues are depression and bipolar disorder.

Trauma

You have been through a traumatic event like a car accident, victim of crime, war, rape, serious life changing medical procedure or even a near death experience. Even though the event is stressful you don't feel you processed it yet, you have flashbacks as if you are reliving the event, feel your nerves are fraught or you just don't feel yourself anymore.

Relationships

Relationship issues include difficulty forming relationships, affairs, betrayal, abuse, sexual intimacy issues, communication and trust issues, separation and divorce, family issues and parenting conflicts. Relationship issues can be worked on in therapy either individually, in couples or within families.

Psychosexual Issues

Sexual issues which have a psychological basis to them such as loss of libido, fear of sex, painful sex, premature ejaculation, erectile dysfunction and performance anxiety.

Psychotic disorders

Psychotic or psychosis disorders involve distorted awareness and thinking. Two of the most common symptoms of psychotic disorders are hallucinations -- the experience of images or sounds that are not real, such as hearing voices -- and delusions, which are false fixed beliefs that the ill person accepts as true, despite evidence to the contrary. Schizophrenia is an example of a psychotic disorder. It is common for these types of issues to be treated with medication alongside therapy.

Addictions and Habits

Addictions can develop from many activities, including drinking alcohol, taking drugs, eating, stealing, gambling, gaming, social media, work, having sex and using the Internet. Often addictions begin as a result of how these activities make people feel emotionally and physically. These feelings can be pleasurable - triggering a powerful urge to carry out the activity again to recreate this 'high'. This can develop into a repetitive cycle that becomes very hard to break, affecting how you feel about yourself, personal responsibilities and relationships. Equally there are other habits with negative impacts, which can include self-harm, hair picking, excessive scratching or biting nails.

Eating Disorders

Eating disorders involve extreme emotions, attitudes, and behaviors involving weight and food. External signs include being seriously underweight, bingeing and purging or bingeing by itself. Anorexia nervosa, bulimia nervosa, and binge eating disorder are the most common eating disorders which can involve underlying feelings of and cycles of stress, worry and shame.

Self-Worth, Identity and Attachment

Usually not separated out as an issue but manifested as part of other problems when you present in therapy. For example you may have low self-worth, which is an opinion you have about yourself and your acceptability and goodness. You may be struggling with identity issues associated with your sexuality, spirituality or cultural heritage and feel something is missing. Sometimes, with *attachment* issues, we can also struggle with fearful feelings of abandonment and rejection as a pattern in life, which can then impair our current relationships, such as the needing to control the other person in case of rejection or loss.

Keyword: Attachment. In a psychological sense attachment issues occur as a result of specific patterns of ingrained behaviors in relation to carers. For example, a child who is not allowed to explore and feel a sense of safety may become insecure. Attachment theory believes some issues with relationships can carry forward into adult relationships, such as excessive distrust of a partner.

Personal Development & Growth

You can be on a journey exploring life, its meaning and your relationship with the world as well as your own beliefs. It's not uncommon for people to explore their own purpose, spirituality, life project(s), ageing, life stages as well as death anxiety. People often want to be the best person they can be whether it's in relationships, community, or being more self-aware of their own conflicts and issues.

Personality disorders

Sometimes people can be diagnosed with a Personality Disorder where people have extreme and inflexible personality traits that are distressing to the person and/or cause problems in work, school, or social relationships. This can interfere with a person's ability to cope in life. Examples include antisocial personality disorder, borderline personality disorder, obsessive-compulsive personality disorder, and paranoid personality disorder.

Psychosomatic Illnesses

You've heard it said that the mind and body are connected and your wellbeing is influenced by both. Although medical issues can't be cured by therapy, the relationship you have with your illness and how it makes you feel, such as your stress about the issue, can be worked on in therapy. People come to therapy to manage medical issues such as cancer, pain, IBS and fertility. Many medical issues can have a stress associated element and thus therapy can help you manage this.

How to spot the psychological signs early

The truth is that most people entering therapy do so when there is a significant or critical issue where they cannot "just wait". Wouldn't it be nice if you had spotted a potential issue earlier and saved yourself a lot of time, money, pain and improved your quality of daily life? For example, people may enter therapy for hearing voices, compulsive thoughts, panic and anxiety or depression. However, when things are slightly off, or it feels you trudge on regardless, these could be some signs where therapy could help you pre-emptively. Here are some ways to spot whether pre-emptive access to therapy could be beneficial.

Remember to check with your physician/doctor in case there are other medical issues involved.

Generally not yourself

What's your norm? You may find yourself feeling angrier and your moods change more than you expect, or it may be that you feel more sadness. Or you may feel more lonely and shutdown. You're just feeling more "off" than normal and what you feel may be uncontrollable or even unexpected. This may combine with feeling fatigued, difficulty sleeping or concentrating.

Engaging steadily in more unhealthy behaviours or substances

You are moving more habitually towards using outside substances or behaviours as a way of coping and feeling better. This maybe in the form of alcohol, drugs, food, sex, self-harming. You may feel you're moving more into a cycle where it feels it would be difficult to let go of the need.

Self-care doesn't work

You're feeling rundown, tired and your natural rhythm of life and flow is out of synchronisation. So you go for a self-care route to help, after all you've done it before – you take breaks, rest and go on holiday, get support from family and friends. However, you still feel fatigued, run down, have difficulty concentrating, sleeping and something does not feel right.

Stressful events

There are so many generic life events that sometimes come up, from bereavement, loss of job, financial worries, divorce, or even to moving house. If you feel a weight of baggage associated with life events such as guilt, shame, and fatigue coupled with no space or time to care for yourself, therapy could be a good option.

You lose interest

Have you stopped doing the activities you ordinarily enjoy? This may be social life, work or a hobby you once enjoyed. If so, ask why? Many people find that emotional experiences, low mood and difficult events keep them from participating in life activities.

Traumatic event

You have been through a traumatic event like a car accident, victim of crime, complex bereavement, war, rape, serious life changing medical procedure or even a near death experience. Even though the event is stressful you don't feel you've processed it yet or you may feel your nerves are fraught or just don't feel yourself anymore.

Impartial Outside support

Sometimes we can feel confused, don't know what direction to take and need to make an important decision. You may have people around to support you. However, it's hard to think straight if you have no one to talk to or have people that are giving you mixed messages and after all they may have an agenda. For example, you are trying to make a decision to move abroad but your family want you to stay and you can't think straight and feel guilty. Therapy can provide a safe space for you to explore your feelings, understand where they come from, resolve conflicts or confusion and make decisions.

Understand yourself better

For some people, therapy is an opportunity to grow by becoming more aware of themselves. There may be things about your history, spirituality or identity that you want to explore, or you want to understand why you made a decision or even what stops you achieving your life goals. Understanding why we think, act, and feel the way we do can be extremely empowering. That understanding can lead to insight, which once out in the open, can channel how you want to direct your life now and in the future.

Faltering relationships

If you're feeling more and more disconnected with your partner and seem to have lost feelings of trust or are developing anger, jealousy, possessiveness and resentment. You may also find it hard to resolve conflicts or make plans for the future. Rather than wait for things to get worse relationship counselling could be used to restore and understand what is going on behind that feeling of distance between you. Remember this can equally apply to family, between siblings, and parent to child or even friend. You can invest time into the relationship to get your needs met and relationships back on track.

Why does therapy work?

So, you're in the therapy room. You sit, you talk and you're listened to attentively with empathy and acceptance. Depending on the type of therapy, the therapist may offer their thoughts and feelings as well as employing a number of different techniques. You would be forgiven for asking, "How can this possibly work?" and "Surely if it were that easy, anyone could do it." Part of the confusion could be because you perceive the therapist to do actually very little; there may be less structure or no fixed roadmap to get you there. Well, I hope in this section to demystify why therapy works.

In his book *Why Therapy Works* (2016), psychologist Louis Cozolino provides a detailed explanation of how and why therapy works from a neuroscientific perspective. I have summarised these as five fundamental ways the therapy process works: by understanding yourself better, by establishing a better relationship with yourself, by experiencing and connecting with your thoughts and feelings, by social bonding, and by moderating fear. Not that all are mandatory for the therapeutic process to be beneficial, but they do reveal what goes on within to effect change. Underpinning that change is our innate mental capability to find imaginative ways to express thoughts and feelings (the unfettered mind) and the innate ability for our brains to develop new mental paths (neuroplasticity).

Understanding yourself better

When you attend therapy, there may be any number of problem areas you're working on, such as an inability to make relationships or to manage difficult feelings, or a general sense of something wrong. Particularly where these issues become a pattern or are repeated as a general way of being, the reasons for them prevailing may remain out of awareness to our conscious minds. Through the safe process of therapy, where you mind is allowed to explore you inner world freely, these more unconscious experiences can be brought out into the therapy room to see how they play a part in your current problems.

Keyword: *The **unconscious,** also called the subconscious, is the set of mental activities within an individual that occur without awareness. Therefore, the unconscious can affect the patterns of a person's behaviour, thoughts, and feelings. Therapy can reveal the unconscious through talking and expression. Some believe that the unconscious can also be revealed in dreams, body language or even slips of the tongue.*

For example, although not always necessary, therapy enables revisiting of your childhood experiences to form new narratives and understandings towards your past. Through this process, you can understand the long-lasting effects childhood has had upon you, including your beliefs and behaviours. By allowing for new perspectives to be formed, new possibilities may awaken inside. These insights can begin to shift unhelpful unconscious patterns you may have learned from the past. Therapy allows exploration, self-understanding, and self-reflection to facilitate change within.

Improving your self-relationship

Self-worth is how you judge yourself. While there are external things like work satisfaction that can build your self-worth, the type of self-worth that people often have difficulty with is self-judgement, which is not tied entirely with external achievements such as personal success, wealth or being appreciated. Self-worth is a deeper sense of judgement and feelings about yourself, such as feeling damaged, unworthy of love, abandoned, or self-loathing. These themes can remain static, having been "created" in our history of childhood, social, cultural, family relationships, school and society. For example, feeling secure with parents and being able to explore and make mistakes is going to be positive for your self-worth, but being persistently scolded, abused, bullied and feeling a lack of belonging in the world is not a recipe for creation of good self-worth. Therapy gives you the skills to reality test maladaptive beliefs, behaviours, and emotions in order to reappraise your worth now. Through the care of the therapist, you can reinstate your sense of self-worth by accepting yourself more and changing the judgements you have towards yourself, thereby restoring a sense of "okayness."

Keyword: Reality test is the objective evaluation of a belief, thought or feeling. For example, you may assume a colleague at work is ignoring you, but there may be many other explanations, such as them having a lot on their mind.

Experiencing yourself

Ever heard the phrase "What does your heart tell you?" "What are your feelings?" or even "Don't just think - feel!" Contrary to popular belief, this is not about making you cry, although that is one possible effect. It simply means not only thinking, analysing and interpreting, but also being in emotional contact with what is and has happened by using the language of emotions. That process can bring out emotions, even anger and sadness, where the thoughts and emotions come together in an experienced reality. Therapists often talk about felt response or visceral reaction; it's as if the body has connected both head and heart. It's not just a rational response, such as, "I know it was difficult." It's an experience: the body shakes, the emotions come forward into the room perhaps with anger and you feel the emotions through your nervous system. You're connecting your thoughts, emotions and body sensations together to heal.

Sociality and bonding

We are naturally social creatures, and our minds have evolved to connect with others in very useful ways for purposes of survival. We always existed in groups, and forming secure attachments with others is a natural way of destressing, and gaining support, protection and love. The benefits of good relationships to our wellbeing is an unarguable truth. Therapy taps into this innate need as a healing agent, by providing a secure attachment with a therapist. How does the secure attachment form with the therapist? By them offering an accepting, empathic and sometimes deeply relational connection. Through the connection, therapists become attuned to your needs, to what is said and also unsaid, and to establish a tentative theory about what is going on for you. From this place, the therapist gets to feel what it's like for you and uses those feelings therapeutically.

Soothing fear

The amygdala is the part of the brain that detects dangers for the purpose of survival, and can trigger fight or flight mechanisms that are very useful to our survival and to deal with a threat. However, the brain can become sensitised to threats based on past experiences and believe a current situation is something to be alarmed about, when it is not. This may be emotional triggers, spiders, relational patterns, needles or active trauma with flashbacks. Through the secure but challenging environment of therapy, people can work on their thoughts and emotions by gradually confronting these perceived dangers and thus desensitising or inhibiting the fear reflex to a realistic baseline.

Unfettered mind

Allowing your mind to freely express itself is a critical part of healing because it allows you to find out who you are and what's wrong. It enables you to think abstractly and imaginatively to express ideas in novel ways through a combination of language, stories, memories, dreams, metaphors, associations, feelings, body senses and intuition. These inbuilt capabilities can help open up your internal world to discover who you are and what is wrong, which in turn can allow you to drop what is no longer needed and to understand what you now need. Therapy, through the safety of the relationship, allows your mind to freely wander, explore and discover.

Through the safe container of the relationship with the therapist, this inner world can be opened up to explore and imagine the kind of future you would like now. For example, by thinking about what it would be like to wake up tomorrow and have what you need and to visually see what that would look like. Stories create identity and spark the imagination, setting the direction of a new future.

Here is a condensed example of a client allowing her mind to free associate in a creative way.

[Agnes feels alone and is losing hope in her life]

Client: I really feel hopeless; it's like I can't see out of the rubble.
Therapist: What do you see in that rubble?
Client: I see lots of big boulders all around; it's dark and no one is there.
Therapist: Can you describe what you see?
Client: It's dark, and cruel. I don't have the energy to get up, it seems. It's not nice at all.
Therapist: So little energy.
Client: I just need a hand up. If only I could get a hand up.
Therapist: Do you imagine anything, anyone who could give that to you?
Client: Well, my son. I feel so warm and light with him.
Therapist: Is that something you could imagine?
Client: Yes, I can.. He is there for me and cares. {Client shows emotion.} I feel a bit lighter.

Neuroscience
From a neuroscience perspective, the mind is plastic or neuroplastic; like dough, it can be shaped through learning. Neuroplasticity is the brain's ability to reorganise itself by forming new neural connections throughout life. Therapy experientially changes the brain and literally creates new pathways of thinking and feeling in the mind.

There are many examples in this book that show how the process of therapy works where the mind shifts through new insights and felt experiences. These shifts literally create new pathways and reinforce hope and belief to catalyse your process in therapy.

Here are some examples of clients achieving a shift in therapy:

"I don't know exactly what happened. I felt upset a lot of the time during the past few weeks. It was painful but I just feel a bit better. I could not tell you exactly why and how this helped me but it has."

"[Karl was feeling low moods.] Understanding how I was shutting off my feelings about my partner and how that felt for her really helped. I was in a loop with her, which continued to make me feel isolated and uncared for. But taking the risk and saying what I felt just made things so much better between us. I still get low moods but they don't last as long now."

"[Amarpreet's bereavement.] I had put so much focus on feeling guilty for not being there for my mum at the moment she died because I had to go to the bathroom. But I almost forgot that maybe she would have wanted it that way, and it really was not my fault it happened that way. I know we loved each other."

"[Kate was traumatised.] Reprocessing the memory and events and the physical shock of seeing my mum having an affair seems less distressing now. I used to relive the moment so much, but now it's not as stressful. It really feels I can let go now."

Chapter 2 – Getting Started

So by now you've understood what therapy is, what it can be used for and why it works. So having decided therapy is for you, this chapter will help you understanding and assess the various therapy options, the right therapist for you, the therapeutic contract and what to expect in the first session.

In this section, you will be provided with a lot of information about therapeutic options. In many cases, these options may not be relevant to you due to circumstances, and in others cases, you may not know or have a strong feeling of what is right for you. If that is the case, then the "keep it simple" approach is suggested:

Work with a trusted therapist, one who meets country standards and has experience working with your types of problems, whom you feel safe with and who believes the approach you are undertaking with them has potential to help you achieve your goals.

You will also be asked to reflect on your own feelings and needs. This is because therapy is about what works for you; what works for one person may not work for another. Don't worry if you feel you don't know; that is your feeling on the matter and it can be respected. This is very similar to what happens in therapy: your feelings are accepted as they are and you make the decisions that are right for you, regardless of any input from the therapist.

Assessing Therapy Options

In this section I'll give you an overview of considerations to determine the right therapeutic approach and therapist for you. In this section you will:

- Determine your options for access to therapy
- Consider whether you wish short or long term therapy
- Consider whether you prefer a particular approach or method to therapy
- Consider any preference you have for the therapeutic setting

Accessing Therapy

Access to therapy will depend on where you live and any cost constraints. You may live somewhere where there are no or few options for therapy, or where there is a wide variety of options across public, charitable, private, insurance and workplace sectors. Access points may include:

- Public services. You may be in a country where free, albeit limited types of therapy with an upper limit to the number of sessions. For example, in the UK CBT is commonly available for short duration, although other types of therapies such as DBT, EMDR are available depending on the type of problem being experienced. Access may be through a referral (in the UK a doctor) and it may involve being on a waiting list, sometimes for many months.
- Workplace Schemes. You may be part of an organization that offers health insurance that includes therapy. Typically therapy through workplace schemes are short term in nature.
- Charities. You may have local access to therapy services who operate as a charity. The service may be free, operated on a sliding scale based on personal circumstances, or as a lower cost option than private therapy.
- Privately. Private typically means you would be paying for therapy, either out of your own pocket or by an insurer. Private therapy, depending on your location, tends to offer most options, shorter waiting time and flexibility to work longer term. Therapists may operate individually or as part of an agency.

Where you have no suitable local access to therapy you could consider online or phone therapy as an alternative. Where you have a therapist who works or is a citizen of another country they may not be able to offer you therapy due to your country's legal regulation. For example, it is not legal for a UK therapist to offer therapy to US citizens, unless they are licensed to practice in the US.

International Variation: Different countries will have different access options to therapy.

Short vs. Long term Therapy

Therapy can last anywhere from a single session to 5 years or even more. There is no way of determining exactly how much time your healing and recovery will take place. The most you could say is that the type of problem, the number of coexisting problems, how entrenched and severe the difficulty, are associated factors to duration of therapy, but there is no formula.

Therapy differentiates between short-term, or sometimes called brief or time limited, therapy, normally between 6-12 sessions, and long-term therapy. Short-term therapy is generally directed to a single specific goal, which focuses the work. Examples of goals could include managing work stress better, overcome driving anxiety, or improving communication in relationships. Short-term therapy is also an option if you are time or cost constrained or as a way of determining whether therapy is right for you. Where access to therapy is provided by public or insurance providers, they will typically offer you short-term therapy, although there may be exceptions.

Short-term therapy may open up other problems and emotions that you were unaware of prior to undertaking short-term therapy. If you're worried about this, then speak to the therapist. Therapists should be able to offer referrals, options, or suggestions for further help if that is the case.

Long-term therapy is open-ended, where the scope and goals of therapy have no fixed constraints. You may share with the therapist what you would like to work on, but the agenda is fluid and open-ended. There are some issues that might benefit more from a longer-term commitment, such as abuse or addictions.

If you feel you may wish to switch to longer-term therapy from short term, then you can ask what options are available early in the process, and whether the therapist would be able to switch to a longer-term model.

Therapy approaches

As well as finding a therapist, there are a number of therapy approaches, sometimes called modalities, to choose from. Although, in general, it is thought that the overall relational fit, relational quality and experience of the therapist is more determinate of better outcomes, the modality may also be important too.

There are over a hundred different types of therapeutic approaches available and unless you already know the type of therapy you're looking for it can feel like a minefield. Generally Cognitive Behavioural Therapy (CBT), Person Centred, Psychodynamic or Integrative therapies are the most practiced and evidenced therapies available. However, that does not mean they are necessarily the only ones that you should choose, there are many approaches to therapy that may be beneficial.

Your choice of therapy may be limited depending on where and how you access it. If you have a strong preference, you may have to use a private therapist. However, remember that your relationship with your therapist is the foundation of therapy regardless of whether or not a particular approach is important for you. Therefore, if you feel the type of therapy is going to be important you may wish to shortlist prospective therapists from a particular orientation or pick a mixture from different orientations first.

Although there are many therapy approaches, they can be generalised as belonging to one of the six schools or groups of therapy:

Analytical insight-oriented therapies – Therapies such as psychoanalysis, Jungian and psychodynamic theories are geared towards gaining insight into yourself, how you think and act by exploring your experiences as well as making the unconscious conscious. There is usually a focus on childhood experiences and the nature of feelings between the client and therapist.

Humanistic therapies – Therapies such as person-centred, Gestalt and existential therapies emphasise the individual's own natural potential to heal and grow. These therapies deemphasise therapeutic interpretation but rather work with the whole person in an atmosphere of empathy. Humanistic therapists believe people are inherently motivated to fulfil their internal needs and their individual potential.

Cognitive and solution-focused therapies – Therapies such as cognitive behavioural therapy (CBT), solution-focused therapy and EMDR emphasise how thoughts, feelings and behaviours work together to impact your life. They focus more on how you want to be, in the context of the past and your memories, rather than looking deeply into childhood development.

A next wave of cognitive behavioural therapies such as acceptance and commitment therapy (ACT) and mindfulness-based CBT (MBCT) combine principles of acceptance (including mindfulness) into their approach.

Integrative or eclectic therapies – These therapies tend to use different elements of different schools of therapy and apply them in a way that is suitable to the client (sometimes called client centred therapy). With schema therapy, although it theoretically stems from CBT, could be classed as an integrative therapy because it combines CBT, insight-oriented (psychoanalytic) and humanistic (Gestalt) ideas within it.

Expressive therapies – They use creative arts including the body as the central tool for your work, such as art, dance/movement, drama, music or drama. The emphasis is on expression using these art forms, not being good at the art.

Couples, group and family therapies – These therapies are geared towards individual and collective goals. For example, improving relationships, developing interpersonal skills or helping each other's change. While none of these therapies lose individual focus they are more geared towards helping you and others overcome difficulties and function better together. They can also be based on a particular school of therapy above – humanistic, insight oriented, integrative/eclectic or cognitive behavioural. The exception is for family therapy, where you may find therapists trained specifically in *systemic therapy* which looks to help the family understand each other by looking at the whole family system in order to change behaviours and resolve conflicts.

Is the approach important?
The short answer is that it matters when it matters. It may matter because it's more suited to your personality or preferences, or because of the types of problems you're experiencing. You're likely to be met with alternative views depending on who you talk to and your context, so it is difficult to say definitively which therapy type will be best for you and your particular problem(s).

Here are some guidelines for the selection of a particular school of therapy. Remember, this list is not exhaustive and should be seen as suggestions for selection, not a recommendation.

- If you believe that early childhood development and the unconscious, that is the things that you're unaware of, is a driver for your issues, then an insight-oriented therapist, e.g., a psychodynamic therapist, may be appropriate. This therapy may offer more suggestive interpretations of how your problems may have developed and how it relates to your difficulties.

- If you believe by focusing on the present within the context of your history, you can change your thoughts, feeling and behaviours, then cognitive behavioural and solution-focused therapies may be appropriate. You want to focus less on the unconscious or the past, but rather on solutions based on here-and-now problems.

- If you believe that you can, through an empathic therapeutic relationship, work through your problems because you believe in the innate ability of your mind to find its way, then humanistic therapy, such as person-centred therapy, may be appropriate.

- If you believe no one orientation is best, then an integrative therapist who uses a mixture of approaches may be appropriate.

The following types of therapies have been created around specific problems, although not necessarily limited to just dealing with those difficulties:

- If you believe you are suffering because of Trauma or Post Traumatic Stress Syndrome (PTSD) then Eye Movement Desensitization & Reprocessing therapy (EMDR) or Somatic Experiencing may be appropriate.

- If you have been diagnosed with Borderline Personality Disorder (BPD) or Bipolar Disorder then Dialectical Behavioural Therapy (DBT) maybe appropriate. DBT typically involves homework, individual and group therapy.

- If you have been diagnosed with a Personality Disorder then Schema therapy may be appropriate

- If you are having a relationship issue with your partner then Couples Therapy maybe best. If the relationship is an issue either with a partner, sibling, parent or friend, couples therapy can offer a space for you to both work through your relationship difficulties. Relationship therapy may involve individual therapy alongside couple therapy.

- If you wish to have a young child access therapy then a qualified Child Therapist may be appropriate, particularly for children under 11.

- If the whole family is encountering issues as a whole, such as due to individual mental illness, substance abuse, eating disorder, or communication issues, then Family therapy may be appropriate. In family therapy the whole family attends together to work on identified problems. Family therapy sees family as a system that has its own dynamics rather than just individuals.

- If you wish to explore your problems in a supportive group with people who maybe struggling with similar issues then Group Therapy, sometimes alongside individual therapy may be appropriate. Common issues may be explored such as difficulties in forming relationships, patterns of painful relational experiences or addictions. Group therapy offers the opportunity to form relationships, learn about yourself through feedback, and to give feedback as part of the healing process.

- If you are having sexual difficulties that are of a psychological nature then Psycho-sexual therapy may be an option.

Therapeutic tools

As well as talking therapy, therapists may introduce a number of tools into therapy to help with your healing process. The purpose of these tools is invariably to help you explore your thoughts and feelings, learn new ways of being, and deepen your understanding of yourself. If the therapist introduces these tools, you are totally in control if you wish to engage with them or not. You may worry about your competence to use the tools, but it isn't about being "good" at using the tool, it's about using the process of expressing yourself through the tool to heal and grow.

- Drama using theatre techniques for healing. Drama therapy (Psychodrama) is its own modality.
- Role play. Where you and the therapist act out parts to learn about new ways of being, such as development of empathy, conflict resolution, or assertiveness.
- Dance uses mind and body techniques for healing. Dance therapy is its own modality.
- Sand tray work. Use of sand to create concrete manifestation of a client's inner world using sand, water, and miniature objects.
- Pebble work. Use of stones to represent ideas and feelings such as with relationships.
- Cards. For example, emotion cards enable people to understand and express feelings.
- Art is a creative way of expression. Art therapy is its own modality.
- Mindfulness. Mindfulness is the psychological process of bringing one's attention to experiences occurring in the present moment, observing and flowing with it.
- Hypnosis. Hypnosis is a state of human consciousness involving focused attention and reduced peripheral awareness, which it is believed enhances your capacity to respond to suggestions made.
- Animals. Animals such as horses and pets are used in the healing process. Equine or "horse therapy" is its own modality.

- Virtual Reality and computer-assisted interventions; for example, in the desensitization of phobias and fears.
- Music therapy. Music therapy is its own modality.

Therapeutic Settings

Therapy is typically offered at the therapist's organisation or their home office. However, therapy may be also be available in a number of different environments such as your home, in outside spaces, in your work office, or even in a noisier environments. In the digital age, therapy can also be available through a number of mediums as well as classical face to face. This include traditional phone, web cam, email, instant messaging, and internet phone/audio systems.

Sometimes people prefer the convenience of home, phone or online access to therapy, or it may be because it is not easy to visit the therapist's office due to lack of transport, disability or an accessibility need. One reason is safety, people who have suffered a trauma such as a crime could be reluctant to meet someone face to face in private and may be more comfortable working online or in an open public space. In other cases people may have difficulties that prevent them from meeting face to face which is why they are accessing therapy in the first place, such as fear of leaving home, having a phobia of open spaces, or a general social anxiety of meeting someone new. For some therapy can be anxiety provoking so having another medium for accessing therapy can provide a transitory or longer term way of accessing therapy.

Whatever method(s) you choose or negotiate with the therapist it's important that you feel comfortable doing so and feel safe from being overheard, so for example having no one in the house when you are online with your therapist. For online systems, the tools used by the therapist must use secure encryption to protect against interception, which is analogous of minimising the possibility of someone listening in to a room. The other type of threat to online security is through anyone who can potentially access your computer device, whether desktop, laptop, tablet or smartphone. If someone is able to access your device, there is a possibility they could access your files, emails and recordings on your computer or worse still install software called "keylogging" which could record all your messages and sessions in stealth for viewing later on. Whatever method you choose, if safety is a worry talk to the therapist about risks and what protections are in place.

Self-Reflection Exercise

What options do you have for access to therapy? including funding?

Do you prefer shorter and goal directed therapy? Why?

Do you prefer open ended therapy? Why?

Is the option of switching with the therapist you first meet from short to long term therapy important to you? If so ask your therapist whether that is a possibility.

What primary problem(s) are you experiencing? Is it relational, trauma, addiction, personality disorder, focused between you and partner or family?

How do you see the importance and priority between type of approach and relationship with the therapist?

Is there a particular type of therapy approach which appeals and is important to you? Why?

Are you able to gain access to therapists from you preferred approach?

Do you have a preference for types of tools used during therapy? For example, mindfulness.

Do you have any preference for the environment you're going to be in? For example, home or internet.

Are there any risks to being overheard in the environment? For example, access to your computer.

Finding the right therapist

In this section, you'll be able to understand considerations in finding the right therapist for you. In this section you will:

- Understand about therapist professional standards
- Understand what types of qualities to look for in the therapist
- Consider what questions you wish to ask a prospective therapist
- Reflect on your feelings when evaluating your needs for therapy

Therapist Standards

Prior to shortlisting therapists, some basic criteria need to be considered, such as qualifications, insurance, experience, specialism and licensure. Therapists may require a formal regulatory license to practice in some countries while in others there are voluntary membership bodies that assure standards. Regulation by law provides a level of protection to clients because they verify reasonable standards of practice, such as qualification, ethical practice, continuous development, supervision, insurance, as well as offering a complaints procedure. The same can be said of voluntary bodies, however there is no legal basis or centrally governed standard for practice, even though membership bodies may enforce the same criteria for membership as in regulated countries. One advantage of using someone who is licensed or part of a voluntary membership body is that you already know they meet a professionally recognised standard and there is usually a complaints process. Although being licensed or registered with a reputable body provides a level of assurance that therapists meets accepted standards it does not necessarily mean they are the best therapist for you.

Voluntary membership bodies standards may vary quiet a lot. It is recommended you use a therapist for an established and reputable body. This will vary depending on the country you are in. For example, in the UK UKCP, BACP, BPS are recognized and reputable member organisations although there are many others.

International Variation: Each country may have its own regulatory or generally accepted voluntary standards

Therapist Experience

Therapist experience with the problems you are working on is highly desirable but is not always a show stopper and grey areas do exist. On the basis that therapy is generally more about the whole person and the healing process of therapy is mostly a creative process, I would not completely way out someone who is not experienced with your problems. What is important is that they have awareness of the types of problems you are experiencing, contraindications i.e. know of any practices that could be harmful, and some theory – additional specialist skills and experience can certainly be helpful but the foundation of the relationship needs to be in place first without which expertise on its own is unlikely to compensate. Therapists are already ethically obliged not to take clients on who they don't feel they have the background to work with.

The problems and approaches below, although not exhaustive would usually require additional training, qualifications or experience to work with beyond the standard qualification unless of course the training specialised in one of these areas in the first place. For example, a therapist base qualification may already include or be focused on children's therapy.

- Dissociation and Post traumatic stress disorder (PTSD)
- Eating Disorders
- Personality Disorders
- Attention Deficit Hyperactivity Disorder (ADHD)/Attention Deficit Disorder (ADD)
- Autism/Aspergers
- Developmental disabilities
- Young Children (usually under 11)
- Couples, Group or Family Therapy

If you are unsure about standards of experience and qualification for your particular problem you can seek third party advice from various governing and membership bodies that assure standards for therapy.

International Variation: Different countries and regions may use different regulatory or de-facto professional standards of practice.

Relational Considerations

Finding a therapist who meets professional standards of practice and are experienced with working on problems your experiencing, depending on where you are in the world, can be the easier part of finding the right therapist, and in many cases that can be all that is needed. You do a search, find someone who meets the standard and has experience of working with the types of problems you are experiencing, you meet them and the rest is history as they say.

However, like a good foundation for a building, the whole therapy process is built upon your relationship with your therapist. What happens if you aren't so lucky, don't find the right therapist or even keep seeing a number of therapists and just cannot find "the one". For many, you'll be working long term with a therapist on very complex and deep wounds where the quality of the relationship comes very much to the fore. The mantra most therapists would adhere to is "it's the relationship that heals". After all, regardless of the experience and qualifications of a therapist, someone who you don't gel with or does not appear to fully understand your perspectives, can put you on shaky ground for recovery. You should therefore spend time on the question "how did the therapist make me feel?" and in doing so whether you feel you can establish a good, safe and trusting relationship with them. But how do you do that you may ask? While there are not guarantees that you will meet the "right one", just like meeting a potential partner for the first time, this section looks at the personal traits and signs to help you assess your feelings.

Relational Styles – Analytic vs Cognitive vs Humanistic

Before making a judgement of what you felt about the therapist, understand that because of the therapists own modality they may seem appear a bit more "aloof", or even distant. For example, a person centered therapist can be perceived as being warmer or relational than a psychodynamic therapist. Although it's very difficult to generalize, psychodynamic or psychoanalytic therapists may appear to give you less in terms of a warmer fuzzy feeling, don't appear to engage in small talk, or disclose anything about themselves, even at a superficial level. This perceived "aloofness" may exist to allow your feelings that are unconsciously held to naturally appear in therapy. While a person centered therapist can appear more personal, familiar and allow you to focus on wherever your mind takes you, a psychodynamic therapist may gently challenge you, for example by bringing you back to focus on things you may be unconsciously avoiding. This is not to say psychodynamic therapists are any more or less empathic and accepting or that person centered therapists don't challenge, but they are informed by their own theoretical modality which influences their relational style, they are ultimately there to work for you in overcoming any problems you present with regardless of modality. For therapies that are more treatment based, short term or structured like CBT, the feeling you have towards the therapist may be somewhere in between the Psychodynamic and Person centered therapist. Again this is just a generalization as individuals ultimately work in their own way regardless of modality, and many aim to work with a person centered relational base regardless of the approach they utilize.

Good enough therapist

The therapist does not have to be perfect or indeed tick all your boxes, but "good enough". I use the term "good enough" therapist throughout this book but what does "good enough" really mean? The phrase "good enough mother" was termed by a british psychoanalyst, D.W. Winnicott. He coined the term to express the idea that while a mother starts by sacrificing her needs to fulfill her child's, such as sleep, later in development the mother allows for small frustrations, for example a delay in responding as the child starts to cry. She is not "perfect" but she is "good enough" in that the child only feels a slight amount of frustration which gives the child space to learn about her place in the world and develop. I refer to the term "good enough" therapist throughout this book to allow for that development, the therapist may not always be attuned to your needs in the room, a good therapist is never able to be "perfect" at all times and know what is going on or what you need, but they can be "good enough" and that is not only realistic but equally may even be an important part of your healing.

Please note that although originally the description was focused on female mother, in the modern setting it is any primary caregiver or caregivers, regardless of gender.

Qualities of a good enough therapist

Overall you should choose someone you feel safe with, who makes you feel accepted and not judged, and who you can foresee being able to create a relationship in which you could disclose whatever you feel you'll need to. Choose someone who feels right for you, as in all relationships not everyone "clicks" naturally with everyone else.

To help you rationally assess the therapist and to continually monitor the therapist's relational quality, I have provided a 6-point rational assessment tool called EPAIY-S you can use to determine how the therapist is with you.

Empathy and acceptance. You feel they listen with empathy and acceptance to what you are saying without judging you. Therapists may challenge or suggest what may be going on for you, but they do so without it being forced upon you.

Presence. On the whole, they are very present, understand what you say, and it feels they are fully with you in the room.

Assuredness. They don't appear to be out of their comfort zone or to be overwhelmed by what happens in the room. This does not mean they are stoic and emotionless, but they exhibit an overall air of confidence. A therapist must only work within what they have training or experience working with.

Inner balance. They work in an emotionally consistent and balanced way with you, even when things are difficult, not progressing, or you're frustrated with them. This does not mean they approve or agree always; they can bring in their perspective, but they work openly with your feelings, rather than shutting them down. Any responses are given in an adult manner that allow therapy to continue, rather than being critical or blaming.

You focused. They keep their focus on you, what you need, and your process. They work in your interest, not their own. Examples include, not using you to share personal life frustrations, helping you to eventually live independently of therapy or referring you on if they do not have the right experience to work with you. They may share personal details but it is still focused on helping you. They also work within agreed boundaries of the service, such as session times.

Supporting factors. They support their practice with self-care, supervision and ongoing self-development as well as having insurance. These factors are external to sessions but reinforce their competence to practice.

These are indications of a good therapist; noting you won't necessarily be able to determine all of these particularly after only talking to them on the phone or after the first session.

- ✓ You felt heard, understood, accepted and not judged
- ✓ You feel they were present in the room, attentive and followed what you said
- ✓ You felt the therapist was open to answering questions, rather than defensive
- ✓ They are accountable. They own their limitations, mistakes and generally are not afraid to be vulnerable
- ✓ They continually work on themselves, improving themselves either personally or their own field
- ✓ They appeared to have a passion for their work
- ✓ You feel seen for who you are rather than only an object with symptoms, issues and labels
- ✓ You felt they were self-aware. They show signs they have worked on themselves through therapy for a significant period of time which indicates they will not enact their insecurities on you and thus provide a "secure canvas" for you to draw on

Here are a few things that may be warning flags when assessing the therapist. When meeting with a therapist for the first time it may be the therapist was just having a "bad day", but you do have to ask yourself whether you want to risk the time, effort and even money particularly when you have other options available.

- × They seem busy, distracted and/or or preoccupied when you're talking to them
- × They don't seem to be fully attentive or appear to fully understand where you're coming from
- × They don't own their own errors. For example, being late or forgetting you told them something significant before
- × Their boundaries are not clear or are brought up in surprise e.g. cost and duration of session, or try to engage in a dual relationship with you e.g. business partnership as well as a therapist
- × They guarantee they can fix the issues
- × They can definitely resolve problems in a certain number of sessions
- × They provide life advice that is unrelated to therapy
- × They have never been in therapy themselves
- × They are judging you and telling you what you're doing wrong or blaming you
- × They spend unnecessary time talking about themselves and their personal life
- × They try to pressurize you into undergoing therapy with them or make you guilty for your issues or not wanting therapy with them
- × They look and respond as if they are tired. Therapists that are overworked or too busy won't necessarily be able to give you the best service
- × They interrupt a lot
- × They don't keep transparent boundaries such as time and cost

I hope you find the right therapist for you, and many do without much effort or hardship. However, many people don't find the right therapist first time and in fact you may take a while to find a good match for you.

Process of finding a therapist
Obviously you can use your intuition but I feel you can really help yourself more if you can meet a number of therapists, ask some questions of your prospective therapist, get to know who they are, their philosophy and really get a feel below the surface. The process of finding a therapist usually involves shortlisting potential therapists, talking with them, asking questions, assessing them and if necessary repeating the process.

Shortlisting possible therapists

Shortlist a few therapists if you can rather than picking the first that comes up so you can compare and contrast. Maybe you'll find a list of potential therapists through the internet which can give you a profile and experience to help, but I would also say not to reserve too much judgement on the profile itself because of our own perceptions of what we see. Some therapists may not be good at the written word so visit or talk to them if possible. Sometimes you can also get a referral or recommendation, e.g., from a doctor or a friend of a friend but don't assume they are the right therapist just on that basis.

TIP: if you use a therapist that someone you know is using or has used in the past consider how you feel about using a therapist who may already know about you through them, also consider if you need to talk about them in therapy. Therapists also may also believe it is in your interest if they know about this especially if they are a current client. I suggest talking about that in the first session so boundaries are understood and concerns clarified.

Many find a therapist through insurance schemes, workplace or public health agencies and are offered a therapist based on availability and/or location. However, even then you could ask whether there is a possibility of consulting with a few therapists, even by phone or email if a possibility. If you have no options but to work with an assigned therapist, but you feel you cannot work with them, an alternative may still be possible.

Talk to potential therapist

When you have a potential shortlist of therapist it is a good idea to talk face to face, although telephone or in some cases online are also good options. Therapists often use voicemail to avoid interruptions during their client sessions, so don't be surprised if you don't reach your chosen therapist straight away. Leave a message and they will return your call. In some cases the initial session maybe provided to you for free or it may be chargeable. The therapist should be clear about any charges for the first session. In the UK you'll find most therapists are happy to chat on the phone for free for a short period.

You can find out whether the therapist feels able to help you with your problem and discuss practical matters such as whether they have appointments at a time and place that suits you and how much they charge. To make a decision I suggest to think about it before making a decision. Other therapists may ask you directly but you should not feel pressured to make up your mind immediately. You can simply ask for time to make a decision, you are free to choose.

Ask questions

If you need to ask questions you should not be afraid to ask them in making up your mind. Therapists should welcome questions. This conversation will also give you a sense of what the therapist is like and whether you would feel comfortable working with them. See the section "Questions for the therapist" for ideas and choose the questions you feel are important to you. I know clients can find asking questions difficult especially if encountering therapy for the first time. This may be due to ideas of politeness or feelings of anxiety, or lack of confidence, some of which you may be coming to therapy for in the first place, but it really pays to ask questions. This feeling of reluctance to ask could also be due to a power imbalance or a preconceived idea of authority, like that of a doctor-patient relationship, or clients may feel that you should not ask questions for fear of causing offence or presuming that they would be seen as challenging or rude to the therapist's authority, but in order to get the therapist you want, I really feel you need to go in and ask questions that are important to you. One way to mitigate this feeling of discomfort over asking questions prior to visiting your therapist is to ask them whether it would be okay to ask them questions including about their life experiences. I think it also is good to forewarn them; you're not looking for them to fail.

TIP: In my experience most clients don't ask any or many questions, ultimately it is all "proof is in the pudding" and that is okay too. If you feel uncomfortable asking questions it's an opportunity to respect your own feelings and you are free to choose.

Assess them

After your first meeting, take a bit of time to reflect upon what you experienced. The section previously on "Qualities of a good enough therapist" provides guidance on assessment. You can also complete the "Self-Reflection Exercise" later in this section.

TIP: If you're embarking on long term therapy or unsure of the fit, you could just take a leap of faith and try out the therapists for three to six sessions before making a decision or even ask for short term therapy. If you can I would recommend this if you aren't quiet sure and have no better options, as the initial session may not be representative of what therapy would be like to work with the therapist and the therapist may be still getting attuned to your needs.

Just like in real life a partnership can eventually be successful even if you're unsure at first.

Repeat

Many people don't find the right therapist first time and in fact may take a while to find a good match for you. If this happens to you, it is not your fault. You have already decided you would benefit from therapy, so it is worth trying again. Also it's easy to assume that you would be using one therapist or approach to recover, but that is not necessarily the case. As with any journey you can meet a number of people along your way.

Questions for the therapist

Generally, you'll be doing most of the talking during the first session, so as well as getting a feel for how they are with you – accepting, empathic and understanding. I recommend asking questions to corroborate how they made you feel. One of the reasons is that it is possible to "imagine" or idealise a therapist based on a kind of perception of the "rightness" of a therapist for you by seeing them as you imagine them rather than as they are. Although you will probably tell them a lot during during that all-important initial consultation, it's more important to recognise how they make you feel. For example, do you get to talk about your needs and do you feel safe, not judged and accepted? These answers can give you some overall clues. So ask yourself on reflection of meeting them: How did they make me feel? It's therefore important to reflect on your feelings in association with the questions that you ask. So really dig deep by asking questions if you wish – ask, ask and ask and you will really get to the bottom of what the therapist's "being" is really like, by checking not just what they answer but how they answer and how it makes you feel. What I want to make clear also is that you should not look for the "perfect" therapist or answers. That is a tall order for any therapist; therapists don't always get everything right, but the qualities of transparency, openness, curiosity and use of themselves are going to be important. That's the "good enough" therapist.

The table below shows possible questions and rationale for why it may be an important question to ask. Choose the ones that are most important to you although I feel Questions 1, 2, 3 are the ones you will always want to ask. As well as these questions you should also remember basic contracting questions like time, frequency and duration (See the section "Understanding and negotiate the contract").

TIP: Some therapists may be reluctant to answer certain question where they feel it would mean disclosing personal information such as "religious affiliation" or "what led them to do therapy", they don't feel comfortable with the disclosure, or because of their therapeutic approach. Hopefully, they will explain why they don't wish to disclose. From experience, this has the possibility bring out feelings of awkwardness, embarrassment or even rejection in clients but hopefully the therapist will handle this well by still being empathic and understanding. If they become defensive and don't handle a well-meaning question you can use that as input into your decision. As a general principle, therapists should always answer questions that are directly relevant to you and the work you are doing, and more reluctant when at the edge between work and personal disclosure. That is not to say therapists will never disclose personal information but they do so in your interests.

Ref	Question	Why it may be important?
1	Do you think you can help me?	Wanting to know whether therapist believes as far as they are aware that they can help
2	Have they worked with these types of issues?	Wanting confidence that therapist has worked with similar issues successfully
3	Are you licensed or part of a membership body that adheres to best practice, ethics and complaints process? And have insurance? And are supervised?	Therapist meets acceptable standards of qualification and ethical practice
4	How do you intend to work with me and my issues?	To understand therapist's philosophy and the way they will work with you. The approach and tools they will use.
5	How do you handle difficult feeling with clients?	If you believe you can exhibit strong emotions in general or towards the therapists such as anger and fear.

Ref	Question	Why it may be important?
6	Do you think you'll be able to work with me long term? If so how long?	You want to feel secure that therapist will be able to work with you long term or you will be very hurt if abandoned by the therapist.
7	How do you understand my problems? And goals?	That the therapist has heard you, paid attention and understands you.
8	What do you think about diagnosis and medication	That the therapist is working with all of you not just labels.
9	How will you keep me safe in therapy?	Worried about confidentiality or you can get relationally hurt if you get too close to someone.
10	What is your confidentiality and disclosure policy? How will I know what I can safely share?	You are worried that something you wish to talk about may need to be disclosed outside of therapy
11	How will I know when it's time to leave? How long will therapy last? How will we review progress? How do you work with endings?	Wanting to understand review, feedback and ending process
12	Do you follow Pre-Trial therapy guidelines?	To ensure that the therapist works within guidelines so not to jeopardise a pending case you are involved in.
13	What do you do if you cant work with someone or need to refer someone on? What areas of mental health would you not work with?	They will only work with you because they can and understand limits.

Ref	Question	Why it may be important?
14	Will you have time and energy for me?	They are able to have time and energy for you in the room. For example, they may mention self care or ensuring less than 20 client hours per week. **Note that some therapist may be reluctant to answer this question due to personal disclosure.**
15	What led you to do therapy?	Can get a feel for therapist's journey and life experience. **Note that some therapists may be reluctant to answer this question due to personal disclosure.**
16	What do you do to develop yourself and your learning?	Therapist continuously learning is important to you. For example, signs a therapist is working on new things may mean they avoid stagnation, keep up to date with mental health problems and are aware of themselves. **Note that some therapists may be reluctant to answer this question due to personal disclosure.**
17	How much time have you spent in therapy?	They understand themselves so understand and creates confidence on their maturity. **Note that some therapists may be reluctant to answer this question due to personal disclosure.**

Self-Reflection Exercise

Before embarking on finding the right therapist consider your needs:

- Do you understand what to do to check if a therapist meets minimum standards for practice in your country?

- What important qualities do you want from your therapist? For example, warmth, respected, seniority, reputation, status, authoritative, and direction giving.
- What do you need in order to trust the therapist?
- Do you have things you want to talk to the therapist about that you are worried may have to be disclosed by the therapist?
- Are you part of a legal trial?

And then reflect on your own perceptions about relationships:

- Are relationships important to you in life? What type?
- What is your ideal type of friend? Or partner?
- Do you make connections with people easily?
- Do you feel you struggle to make connections with people?
- Do you often feel disappointed with relationships? If so why?
- Do you generally find after meeting a number of therapists you cannot feel a connection with the therapist even after several attempts? Why do you believe that is? Are there any parallels between how you feel with therapists and other relationships?
- Do the answers to these questions change what qualities you look for in a therapist?

So you've met one or more therapists and there will be an exchange of information. To make a decision I always ask my prospective clients to think about it and let me know. Although you will probably tell them a lot during that all-important initial consultation or call, in making a decision it's more important to recognise how they made you feel.

You can reflect upon:

- Did you feel comfortable with them and talking about yourself to them?
- Can you imagine being able to talk about the things you want to talk about freely or eventually when you're ready?
- Were they accepting and non-judgemental of you, your issues and did not make you feel guilty or ashamed?
- Did you like their character? For example, were they open and honest when asking questions?

- Were they attentive, present and they understand you? Therapist need to give you 100% in the session so you should feel as if they are present in the room.

All competent therapists must adhere to ethical as well as competence standards when working with you. You have a lot of power and rights, here are the most significant rights, although there are many others too:

- Be treated fairly, with dignity and respect
- The therapist puts you as their primary concern
- You can ask questions about anything related to your therapy. For example, the way they are working with you and why they made a decision to pause or end therapy with you.
- Expect the therapist to be professional and competent. They only work with you if they can and within their limits.
- Right to privacy and confidentiality unless harm to yourself or others is a concern
- Freedom to say "yes" or "no" to methods employed in therapy and ultimately therapy itself
- Freedom to talk or not talk about anything
- To know what information is kept about you, usually with initial consent, and copies provided on request
- To have access to a complaints process

Typically your responsibilities are no more than turning up, paying for sessions, providing any essential information required, and not to physically harm the therapist. There may be other responsibilities depending on the therapist or the organization. Essential personal information you provide may vary, but it could be as little as your name, doctors and contact details.

Having a lot of rights that does not mean the therapist does not have a right to refuse something you suggest, it is collaborative after all. For example, referring you on is based on putting you first as their primary concern.

International Variation: Each country may have its own regulatory or generally accepted ethical standards

Disclosure

Before you meet the therapist, be mindful that, although therapy is confidential, there are limits to what the therapist can keep to themselves without talking to someone else. In most cases, the therapist will tell you if they are thinking of or will need to disclose material. Disclosure may be to a doctor or another support service, law courts, social services, or even the police.

Therapists tend to use a catch-all statement: "I have to disclose if I feel you or another person maybe at serious risk of harm," which can specifically include though is not limited to:

- Harm to a child or vulnerable adult through abuse, including neglect, sexual, financial, or physical abuse. This is not limited to children in your family but can be any child that you discuss.
- Serious criminality including terrorism and money laundering.
- Legal trial. If the therapist is asked to take the stand as a witness, they will be subpoenaed and therefore cannot hold matters in confidence.

Therefore, there are limits and, contrary to popular myth, therapists are compelled just like anyone else to testify in a law court if mandated. If you are worried about disclosure, you can ask the therapist at the initial session (or any subsequent session) what their stance to disclosure would be.

International Variation: Each country may have its own regulatory or generally accepted disclosure standards

The First Session

Congratulation! You're ready to meet your therapist. The first session, sometimes called the initial session, consultation or initial assessment is there for both you and the therapist to determine if you are a good fit for each other. You'll figure out if the therapist is right for you and the therapist will figure out if they believe they can help you.

Here are some things you can do to make the most of your first session.

- ✓ Read through this section and identify anything that may be relevant to understand or discuss at the first session.
- ✓ Be ready to state what is "wrong", your thoughts and feelings. If you feel you will struggle you can always write it down and take it with you.

- ✓ Inform the therapist if you have any significant needs. See the section below.
- ✓ Inform the therapist of the ways you like to learn. For example, if you're neurodiverse, you may prefer visuals rather than working with feelings.
- ✓ Ask questions if you wish. You can ask about the therapist, their philosophy to determine if they are right for you. See the section "Questions for the therapist" for ideas.
- ✓ Be open and honest about your feelings. Remember the "good enough" therapist will accept you as you are in the room. They offer a safe and non-judgmental environment and work with you "as you are".
- ✓ Remember that therapy is a process and is not generally considered a fast fix.

Informing of significant needs

Prior to meeting your therapist you may hold concerns even before you meet them, for which you can make preparations or ask questions before hand.

Some immediately practical concerns reporting by clients include:

- Does the room have access to nearby toilets?
- Do the facilities have disabled accessibility?
- Whether access is discreet, or via a waiting room? In some cases you may be asked to wait in a waiting room with others, in other settings your hardly ever going to meet anyone prior.
- Is the place safe? For example, will there be other people in the building. Sometimes clients can feel safer during the day with people around, while others prefer that no one else is around.
- Having an emotion or fear triggered. For example, fear of being alone with the therapist and trigger words or situations that cause flashbacks or phobic reactions.
- Don't feel you'll be able to talk at all to the therapist. The therapist may be able to assure you or find a tool to help with your expression, such as art or emotion cards, which provides a different activity to talking that does not need you to be intensely focused on the face to face encounter.

TIP: if your anxiety or fear is of concern you may wish to take a trusted person with you, they can wait outside or by agreement with the therapist allowed into the initial session so that you can get more comfortable.

While the therapist will not be able to control everything, but at least you will be forewarned in what to expect and the therapist can learn about any significant things you're worried about prior. If you have any particular concerns or needs you can ask the therapist prior.

What to expect at your first session

Therapists tend to have different approaches to assessment for the first session. The session may be totally open ended, with no or only a few questions are asked, and you just talk as you wish about what is going on. Alternatively the assessment may be more prescriptive, where you're asked a list of questions which they complete in front of you, or even ask you to complete a questionnaire before or during the session.

Unless you are there with a therapist who is skilled in diagnosis, and that is what you want, therapists won't diagnose you. Mental health diagnosis can only be carried out if they are qualified to do so, typically the field of psychiatry and clinical psychologists, and would likely to be over an extended time or a number of hours or sessions. Either way, as a minimum they will want to understand why you are seeking therapy, any symptoms you are experiencing and some background. If you feel you will find it hard to express these you may wish to take some notes with you to provide, read or explore with the therapist.

Here are some questions that you are likely to need to explain or respond to at the initial session:

- Why are you seeking therapy? What issues and symptoms are you experiencing? For example, because of a bereavement, feeling low or work stress.
- What impact does the issues cause you? For example, your problem might be causing difficulty at work, sleep issues or panicky feelings.
- What your expectations of therapy and the therapist? For example, you may only have time for set number of sessions or want more direction from the therapist.
- What you have already tried to help yourself? This may include past therapy.
- Some information about your background. For example, when your problems started, previous history of problems or even a description of

your family constellation (which is to understand where you fit in your family relationships)

Of course the initial session is an opportunity to assess the therapist and ask questions. See "Questions for the therapist" to assess what is important to you.

Also If you have any concerns about the counselling contract such as disclosure and record keeping that can be explored at the first session (See the section "Understand and negotiate the contract").

During or towards the end of the session, the therapist is likely to indicate whether or not they could work with you, if not a number of reasons may be given (See the next section "Why a therapist may not be able to work with you"). The therapist may then ask you to think about it and let them know if you wish to continue, while other therapists may ask you directly whether you wish to continue. You should not feel pressured to make up your mind immediately, you can simply ask for time to make a decision, you are free to choose.

If you decide to begin therapy you may also be asked for personal information such as:

- Personal contact details
- Doctors name
- Next of Kin
- Previous history of emotional or mental health problems
- Current Medication
- Any previous suicidal attempts

TIP: If you are worried about the collection of this information and its purpose you should talk to the therapist. Generally therapists do not share information without your consent or only if mandated (See Disclosure). For example, you may be concerned that by providing doctors information confidential information could end up on your record and be shared with an employer.

Why a therapist may not be able to work with you

In this section I bring together the considerations from a therapist's perspective of why they may not feel they are right for you. Where the therapist appears not to be able to work with you, some may find that in itself stressful and feel failure or rejection, however you should bear in mind that the therapist is working in your interests so there will be reasons for their decision. It may feel like a rejection and that can be discussed with the therapist or your next one, but to look at it another way it shows that the therapist is being ethical and kinder to you by being realistic and knowing their limits. Therapists come from a range of backgrounds, experience and personal perspectives so all therapists will naturally have different perspectives and opinions on whether they can help you. It's no one's fault, this is a stepping stone in your journey and you can learn from it. In most cases therapists may be able to offer a referral and signpost alternative services that may cater for your needs.

Expertise and level of experience

A therapist may simply be unable to work with you due to lack of expertise and experience. Typically the more severe and distressed a client, the more a therapist will consider whether they have the internal resources to work with you. For example, therapists without sufficient experience in working with young children, psychosis and schizophrenia may feel that you will not be served best by them. It is not necessarily the case that more serious mental health issues are the issue, it may be that the therapist has chosen not work in certain areas due to their own self-understanding and limits. For example, a therapist may have decided not to work with addictions because of similar issues they experienced with a caregiver growing up.

Meeting expectations

A therapist may not wish to take you on because they cannot meet your expectations. This could include basic needs around timing, duration and frequency of sessions, or could be based on whether they can meet your expectations of the outcome. For example, you may have a limited number of sessions you can attend to achieve your goals and they don't feel it's realistic. Some therapists may believe that they can't help you because of these constraints while others would be freer to work with you within those constraints, leaving you to decide what is best. Either way the therapist should be open about whether they feel they can meet your expectations.

Relational Issues

apist is trained to provide you with a safe and impartial zone where
he therapist can work untainted by outside interference. If they
know of you previously or know someone else who knows you that is likely to
be a reason for not working with you. Another reason could be they have
worked or are working with someone you know. Other times it may be that
you are in close proximity, such as neighborhood, inside a community or club
setting. You and the therapist will need to consider whether this will interfere
or make things awkward. Feeling awkward in therapy is not what anyone
would want as it can interfere with talking about feelings and disclosure
openly.

Therapists that work with groups or couples also may consider the dynamic of
working with people for the same reasons. In addition, they will carefully
consider whether they can work with you in multiple settings, such as
individually and then within a couple. The reason for these boundaries is in
order to create an impartial safe place where you're both able to work
unfettered from unnecessary interference.

Agency Policies

Some public services, workplace and insurance providers assess you prior to
agreeing to take you on as a client and thus actually seeing your allocated
therapist. The provider may have their own set criteria prior to taking you on.
For example, an agency may not take you on if you're under 18, or if the
problem is related to substance or domestic abuse. This can sound unfair, but
it will be to do with economic, risk or scope by which the organization
operates.

Understand and negotiate the contract

So once you start therapy you'll agree to what is usually termed a therapeutic
contract. It provides an agreement of how you will work together. Usually
clients will accept the agreement, but if you need more flexibility in the
agreement it may be worth understanding it further and talking this through
with the therapist, particularly at the initial session. Most therapists are likely
to have a written or electronic contract for you to read and perhaps sign, while
others state their contract verbally. The scope and content of the contract can
vary from therapist to therapist, but here are some consideration.

TIP: Remember if anything is unclear to you there is no reason why you can't
ask for clarification.

Timing

As well as looking at your time and day availability you can also consider your best mental timing. What you want is to be engaged and be mentally alert as far as possible, certainly you don't want to be tired. On the flip side, you may be tired after therapy and going to work may be difficult. For example, if you are going to therapy at 8am can be beneficial because you have more energy.

Frequency

Typically therapy is conducted face to face once a week for 50 or 60 minutes. However, if you or the therapist feel more or less sessions are needed, that can be discussed. Sometimes clients may be under severe distress, for example from trauma or grief so you may wish to have more therapy. Sometimes therapists may be able to offer a tentative backup slot so that it can be used if really needed. Further it may be that you feel a long session would be beneficial, 60 minutes or even 90 maybe possible as long as both you and the therapist are able to agree and work effectively for that duration. It is not uncommon, for example for EMDR therapy to last 90 minutes at a time.

Fees and cancellations policy

The contract should clearly state the fees and the cancellations policy. Some therapists may offer free, low cost or reduced rates based on a sliding scale and you can confirm these with the therapist.

Method and Scope of Delivery of therapy

Most therapy is conducted face to face at the therapist's office. As discussed other settings for therapy including online, phone or even outdoors may be possible. While most therapists only work at allotted times with you they may allow you to express feelings in between sessions, such as via email. Regardless of the method the contract should state the boundaries of the service provided. For example, DBT therapy may involve individual sessions as well as phone coaching for help in between sessions. In addition, clients and therapists may have the option to mix a number of delivery methods. For example, it's not uncommon for clients to want to be able to securely message the therapist and this may be something that can be negotiated by exception, but with clear boundaries such as the frequency and time to respond.

Session Recordings

No recordings are allowed to be made in therapy unless you give prior permission or its part of the contract you agree to. Therapists may request recordings be made for various reasons including to gain help in supervision, reflect on the case, research or to record a case study for training and development. Remember that in all cases you have a choice whether you wish to do so. If you do provide permission you should understand the purpose, who it will be shared with and how and when the recording is to be destroyed.

Be clear on what therapy you're receiving

You may be wanting a particular therapeutic approach or use particular tool, so be clear on the type of therapy you will be receiving. For example, if you were expecting EMDR make sure that is clear. Some therapist, particularly integrative therapists, may use a range of orientations, but if you wanted to focus, say, more on CBT, clarifying that with your therapist will help you get off to the right start. Of course the therapist may have an alternative view, but that is one you can discuss.

Confidentiality

To work on the issues you want to work on, and disclose information you need to, it could be worth considering how safe is safe and the limits of confidentiality and disclosure. Therapists usually have a clause about keeping things confidential, unless they are legally bound or there is a risk of harm to yourself or others. What this typically means is that therapists are duty bound to report children's safeguarding issues, terrorism and money laundering. It is also a myth to think that a therapist is in a privileged position and even if they were subpoenaed to court they would plead "sorry sir, that's client and therapist confidential". The reality is that therapists can be asked to give evidence or support a case, so there is a limit to confidentiality.

Pre-Trial Therapy (PTT)

If you are going called as a witness in an upcoming trial you need to inform your therapist at the initial session. Before undertaking therapy you should discuss this with your legal team and the prosecution prior to starting therapy to ensure it does not impact on the case. In many cases you may need to seek permission. The reason is that as a witness your evidence may be vital to a case, and if you are undertaking therapy, or where the therapist does not work with you within PTT guidelines it could jeopardies the case. In addition, the therapist may need to prepare specific notes about therapy and they could themselves be called as a witness to a trial. Although therapists may not have a statement in their contract regarding PTT, it needs to be brought up by you for this reason.

TIP: Ask the therapist what guidelines they follow in working with you if you are going to trial. For example, the therapist is not to ask leading questions about the crime or ask you to reprocess it.

TIP: Prosecution services generally prefer you to undertake non-directive approaches to therapy such as person centered therapy, rather than more directed approaches like psychodynamic therapy.

Similarly, if you are being prosecuted or bringing a case against someone the same principles of telling the therapist apply so that nothing is detrimental to you.

Record Keeping

Therapists vary in their approach to confidential record keeping from just keeping appointment dates/times to more detailed factual information. In country rules and legal requirements will need to be following by the therapist for the handling, processing, sharing and destruction of personal information. If you are concerned about recording keeping discuss that with the therapist. In most countries you will have a right to get access to any information stored about you, what it shall be used for, how it is handled, modified and destroyed. For example, in the European Union GDPR consent has to be provided by clients to store personal information.

Custom Records and Reports

If you need the therapist to keep records in a particular format, produce assessment reports or letters produced you should convey this up front, so the therapist can determine whether they can meet your needs. This applies equally if you are looking for letters and records to be produced for use by other organizations, such as doctors, work, courts, probation services and social services. There is always also a possibility that the therapist may not be able to meet your needs so it's always best to check.

Contact boundaries

Makes clear allowable contact between you and the therapist. Most therapists only work at the allocated timing and are not operating a crisis line. However, some may work with you within limits such as allowing messages between sessions. It is important to note the therapist relationship is different to a friendship and certainly would not extend outside of therapy. Therapists also don't connect with client's online and social network platforms.

About the therapist

A statement of the therapist's background, qualifications, membership to any standards body or licensure, insurance, complaints process and approach to therapy. This will provide confidence that the therapist meets requisite standards of practice.

So now you have begun therapy, you'll want to get the most out of it. Here are some of the fundamental ways in which you help yourself to get the best out of therapy.

Prioritisation and Commitment

There is no doubt the more committed you are to your healing process the more likely you are to see results just like any goal, dedication can pay off. Commitment can be a range from turning up regularly, using all the time available, being really present and wanting to engage in the process. In the fast paced lives we live in, with the desire for continuous production, productivity and progress it is all too easy to add one more item called "therapy" into your busy lifestyle. If you already have a workload full to the brim or overflowing, therapy itself, because there is a time commitment, ends up taking a backseat or becomes another tick in the box activity of life. Ultimately, it may be that you don't have time yet. So really consider whether you have the energy, time and priority to give to therapy. If not, look to see if other things can wait and be honest about your reasons for not being able to prioritise therapy. For example, is it because of money, don't like the therapist, feel scared of the problem and what will spill out in therapy or you're not ready to change yet.

Be Open and honest

Be as open, honest and vulnerable as you feel possible about your problems, and if appropriate the relationship you have with the therapist. Therapy is an opportunity, sometimes the first time in people's lives, to talk about whatever they feel. Through that process the therapist can do the best work for you and you learn that you can be more of yourself in the room. Remember therapy is supposed to be a safe space where the therapist is not there to judge and what you believe may be impolite is welcomed in to the session. If you do feel this is difficult you can ask for the therapist for help, say, by being open and honestly saying that "you need help to open up".

TIP: If you need to say something but feel it would be too difficult face to face then secure email or messaging is an option

Take charge

In and out of the therapy take charge of the healing journey you're on. Taking the lead is vital as the change comes from you and your perspective or inner *frame of reference*. The therapist is not the expert on you; you are and you know ultimately what is best for you. Certainly don't expect the therapist to do all the work and talking, it's a collaboration and you're the driver and the therapist is the active passenger to help you.

Get in the zone

When you go to sessions you can help yourself by having your mind in the zone. Everyone knows what works best for them to get their mind engaged in therapy. You may want to arrive early or avoid certain times in the day for therapy sessions. For example, going to therapy in the middle of a work day maybe absolutely fine for some but be a distraction for others. Ask yourself whether your mind is in therapy when you are in session rather than distracted. You may be constrained by the time and that is okay too, unless of course it is causing therapy to stagnate or be harmful to you.

Use therapy as a practice for life

This means that if you're struggling with aspects of life you can safely experiment with airing them in the therapy room. So for example, if you struggle to share feelings towards people, share them with the therapist. If you struggle with conflict resolution, bring it up and see if you can resolve it. You don't have to wait, you can even ask if the therapist can role play some of the scenarios you are working on.

Recognise the new in you

Recognise in yourself changes that occur so you can be consciously aware of your results, the benefits of therapy and so stay motivated. For example, being more assertive at work, more in touch with your needs, or even socialising, or having more energy for life. These milestones can be cause to celebrate too.

Give feedback

If you want the best from your therapist, it's just like working collaboratively in any field. Help the therapist help you by giving them feedback on what works, what doesn't and if possible your feelings about what you may need.

Educate yourself

Learn to educate yourself, sometimes called psychoeducation. So for example, learning about trauma, anxiety, panic attacks, and depression and what causes them not only empowers your understanding of what is going, but helps you also understand you're not alone. If you found this book helpful, why not follow my blog, join the "Empowering you therapy" Facebook group, or read one of my other books that delve in to the therapeutic process once you begin therapy.

Don't let therapy override life

It's tempting when the pandora's box of emotion starts coming out that all you want to do is to heal and improve quickly, and so put as much of your time and energy into it as possible. You may start reading more, thinking more, going to therapy, but find that everything else in your life gets left behind including important relationships and your own self-care. Because therapy could make you feel worse before feeling better self-care may be even more important. It's important to recognize that therapy is for living your life and therapy wont in itself be enough to sustain all your needs. That does not mean pushing through when you are distressed or just can't cope, but seeking the support and time you need. Everything in balance.

Chapter 3 - Client matters: Beginning Therapy

This chapter addresses consumer concerns (as highlighted in "Your concerns answered") that have not been addressed. The content of this book is based on gathering information from hundreds of clients about their concerns as they approach their first session. Overall, there are three categories of concerns people have before they enter therapy. First, there are suitability concerns about whether therapy will work and if the fit with the therapist will be right. Second, whether they will be able to fulfil their role in therapy to do what is needed. Third, the impact therapy will have on their lives.

If you are interested, I have collected statistics in Appendix A which show the most common concerns that clients have. This may help you understand that any concerns you may have are really normal.

Encounter concerns

Concerns about the encounter with a therapist can range from feeling worried about being alone with the therapist, being judged or made to feel you are wrong, to feeling that the setting of therapy is just too intimate. Being nervous about therapy is very normal, especially if it's your first time and you have not been used to talking about yourself before.

If you feel you can, I recommend talking about these feelings with your therapist. They can lead to important new areas of exploration, insight and collaboration to see what can be done to help you settle your worries so you can get the most out of the sessions.

If you are feeling that you will be judged or made to feel wrong, remember that therapy is not about telling you you're bad in some way or forcing you to do or talk about things you don't want to or telling you that you need to do better in therapy. Therapy is an open invitation for you to be yourself as you are, not as you may believe the therapist expects you to be. Therapy is about providing an accepting, empathic and safe environment for you to work on what you want or need to work on. If you feel nervous about sharing something that you are embarrassed about, those feelings are accepted too and it is quite normal; you can go at your own pace, when and if you're ready. You may *feel* the therapist will judge you or say you are wrong, but therapy is quite the opposite.

You may be nervous about being alone with the therapist or engaging in therapy because of the problems you would like to work on, for example, because of a past traumatic incident, anxiety or phobia. That is perfectly understandable as it could trigger heightened emotional or physical responses that make it difficult for you. Some of these triggers could be because of the gender of the therapist, fear of leaving home, social anxiety, relational problems, or even particular keywords associated with a phobia. If this is the case, you can inform the therapist prior so they can adapt their approach with you, but if you feel it is not an option, you could also consider other access methods, such as online audio, phone or even instant messaging. Eventually, you may feel ready to meet the therapist face to face if appropriate.

If your worry is that you will be asked to talk about things you're not ready to talk about or even that you know deep down you need to at some point, for example, a past abuse, then that is respected. Perhaps you are not quite ready for that, in which case you can even tell the therapist that. Therapy is a process. If you're not ready, you can talk about other important or related aspects such as your family history, stresses and feelings that are present in the "here and now" rather than particular events. The therapist should respect your feelings and not push you to talk about things you're not ready for. If you feel nervous about sharing something you are embarrassed about, those feelings are accepted too and it is quite normal; you can go at your own pace, when and if you're ready. You can also consider talking about feelings such as shame or judgement, or of not wanting to disclose with the therapist and only explore the elements or feelings you are ready to explore.

If you feel you will be blocked, clam up or won't be able to speak in therapy, you may wish to reflect on what you feel is the reason you are anxious about that in particular. Remember, the therapist is the one who is professionally trained and if good enough, they will be able to work with you as you are, as they have likely encountered and worked with a very broad range of client experiences, including complete silence and little expression at all. They may introduce other methods of expression, such as emotion cards, to help you and to give you time and space with empathy and acceptance to allow you to open up gradually in your own time.

TIP: You should also consider whether your anxiety about the encounter could actually be related to what you are trying to work on. For example, you may feel the therapist may judge you because that is how you experienced your own childhood.

Vulnerability concerns

Is your worry about talking about your personal life and in particular showing deeper emotional feelings including anger, sadness or even tears? If so, reflecting on why this is the case in therapy may be useful. For example, is it because you were not brought up in an environment where feelings were expressed? When you tried to express feelings, were you made to feel they were wrong or did no work? Or, is it simply something you're not used to doing? If you had experiences in the past when your feelings were not handled well, understood, validated, accepted and cared about, it can cause you to feel you don't want to share; after all, why would you want to share when feelings are not valued by people around you or when you're made to feel ashamed, rejected or not right? You may have come from an environment of "stiff upper lip" or "boys don't cry," so now, opening up feelings can be a scary thing to do. The downside of this approach is that it can block being able to form deeper connection with people. If you're not ready to trust, it can expose you to hurt, especially if your vulnerabilities are rejected.

As a thought experiment, conjure up the last situation when someone opened up, either to you or you saw the situation in a film or read it in a book. What did it feel like to you? My guess is you would have felt more empathy and you would have felt closer to understanding them. By being vulnerable, if and when you are ready, a better connection with yourself, the therapist and importantly with your own healing in therapy will be created. If it is difficult, try opening up in smaller units first and then move towards what you feel would be more difficult. For example, talk about feeling angry with your partner and then graduate to why it makes you feel hurt inside. This does not mean being unguarded with feelings, but with a good therapist you could begin to see vulnerability as a strength that makes you feel better connected, rather than a weakness.

Performance concerns

After concerns about therapist competence and getting a therapist that is the right relational fit, the most frequent concern is the worry about "doing therapy right." If you're reading this, then I presume you will have picked up some of the ways in which you can help yourself and in particular the section "How to get the most out of therapy."

I believe above all, being you, as you are, is a big part of "doing things right." Therapy is an open invitation for you to be yourself as you are, not as you may believe the therapist expects you to be. By just being you and sharing with your therapist your true feelings, worries about "doing therapy" right, about the therapy process or about the therapist, is "doing therapy right" because it encapsulates a number of therapeutic qualities in one swift move. It involves talking about your worries, expressing feelings, allowing the relationship to deepen through understanding, letting the therapist know something about you, asking for help, as well as opening up the possibility of new insights that may directly link to the problem you are trying to resolve.

Therapy may also make you feel that you have to perform well, like a "good client" or you must know the answers. You may feel internal pressure to perform, or to meet the therapist's expectations as well as ultimately to achieve a good outcome. Part of this may have to do with being vulnerable, having difficulty asking for help, feeling less power or feeling you need to be competent and good at therapy. You can reflect on what the need is about in therapy to see if it leads to new insights and whether it links with what you are in therapy for. If you have become aware of these feelings, that's a great step and opportunity. Of course, therapy relies on your commitment to want to work on yourself, but therapy does not intrinsically require a particular standard or ideal for you to be present. It's about working with you as you are.

Not being understood

If you have a concern about the therapist not being able to understand you, remember that the therapist will by nature of therapy be concentrating on understanding your world, which is what they are there for. They will try their best to understand what you are saying, to get into your world and to get to know you and why you feel that way. This understanding is intrinsic to therapy. However, if your worry about being understood comes more from your own life experiences of not being understood, heard, dismissed and invalidated, you can reflect whether that concern is born out of your life experiences.

Of course, it may be that you do feel the therapist does not understand, and you feel the therapist does not get you or is not attuned to what you're saying. These feelings may be occasional blips or you may feel it is a continuous problem. The stage and maturity of the relationship will also be a factor as attuned understanding may not be present yet. For example, you feel they doesn't understand the impact of the session on your wellbeing, they are holding something back or even they are distant (See Relational sideration->Qualities of a good enough therapist). Not only is it possible for this misunderstanding to derail your therapy, it may also be an opportunity for you to discover something related to your problems, particularly as it is thought that any relational difficulties outside of the therapy room can "show up" in the room too.

One way to overcome this is to write down what specifically makes you feel the therapist does not understand and how you feel it is impacting you. Be open to having a conversation with the therapist, listening and taking in what they might say as they may say something that helps with your feelings and the bigger picture of whatever it is you are working on. Although it may feel uncomfortable to talk about your feelings, the discomfort may open new doors in your process. After talking to them, reflect on how the conversation felt to you. Did you feel energised and hopeful? Did it feel neutral or did it make you feel worse? If it does not improve, then moving on could be an option if you feel you're not getting your needs met and therapy is stagnating.

Impact of therapy

Concerns about the impact of being in therapy range from cost of therapy, feeling worse particularly before feeling better, consequences of your change, or finding out something you may not like.

You may be concerned that therapy will cause disruption in life because it may change you, which could cause you to see relationships in a different light. Ultimately, if you are choosing to go to therapy, especially longer-term therapy, there could be changes to you as a result. There is no guarantee that you will not do so, even if you benefit from therapy. However, you are in control. You can decide what you choose to reflect upon or want to change. The therapist will not force you to change or make you talk about things you don't want to talk about. You can reflect upon what aspect of changing concerns you: relationships, lifestyle, the past, your existing view of who you are, etc. That decision can only be yours to make to determine if therapy is worth it. Remember, just because you decide this is not the time to work on something does not mean you can't return to it at a later date.

Similarly, if you are feeling concerned about what you will find out in therapy, say a previous event you're not ready to face, or even a possible diagnosis, although diagnosis is rarely the remit of therapy, you can talk to your therapist about your concerns. For example, you can clarify if it's important to you that you don't want a possible diagnosis or you don't want to talk about childhood issues but only your "here and now" problems. If you feel that some areas may cause you to feel feelings you're not ready to face or want to change, remember you are in control. Talk to your therapist about your concerns.

If you are concerned about feeling worse during therapy, the truth is that can happen, particularly if you are dealing with deeply painful issues. However, it should not feel that you have been re-traumatised as if the past is happening again or to the extent of causing long-term damage. Here you can see the "worse feeling" as having an existing wound opening up to discharge fluid to heal. It could be a sign that you are moving forward in the process. Talk to your therapist if you are concerned about feeling worse during therapy.

Stigma of Therapy

Do you feel very reluctant to enter therapy because of an inner voice that says, "What if someone finds out?", "This is not something we do!", "It's shameful to talk to a stranger about feelings." Or "Only crazy people go to therapy."

It is understandable that you may feel this way because historically, mental illness and mental health and therapy have been treated as something that is shameful, inferior, and a sign of weakness or craziness. If the collective society or family buys into that narrative, then it is self-fulfilling because it can be used as a rationalisation to stop people getting the help they need. Imagine saying to someone, "Don't go to the doctors because your leg is painful." At the extreme, mental health, just like physical health, can kill if left untreated.

Although I am writing from a non-political perspective, a lot of that stigma can be traced back to controlling, hiding shame, secrets and ultimately power. There will be many reasons historically for this stigma to perpetuate, including the fear of outsiders using information against a family or group. This sentiment is perfectly understandable from a survival perspective since "good" and "bad" is determined by a set of rules, and if people found out, those secrets could be used against them. The darker side is that secrets can also give rise to insulating negative behaviours, including abuse. In short, there is a historical background and real-life consequences to receiving emotional help, so much so that the term "mental health" can feel scary, which perpetuates the stigma of seeking help through therapy.

However, now many societies, families and people are moving away from the sentiment of "there is something wrong with you" to "there is something right with you," and therapy can be applauded as an act of self-respect and compassion for individuals and the larger collective human race. That does not mean it is all safe sailing because there is still unfortunately a wide variation of opinions, and stigma does still exist.

Nonetheless, feeing worried about your family, work or friends knowing you are in therapy is still a common position to take. There may be a number of reasons for that. You may feel people may use it against you or you will be asked questions about it that you don't want to answer.

So, how do you mitigate this risk of someone finding out information about your therapy? First, remember the therapist won't force you to talk about anything you don't want to talk about. They won't judge you, but they accept you as you are. Remember that therapists abide by a code of ethics which includes a confidential agreement; they are not allowed to talk about your matters with anyone, including family, unless it is of a serious concern (see section on Disclosure). Even if a therapist talks about you to a supervisor, they won't reveal any identifying information, e.g., your name.

Second, if you are worried about people finding out you're in therapy, talk to your therapist and assess the risk. Of course, there is always a risk of bumping into someone and some places may have more risk attached to that because of the amount of people moving through the environment or some counselling agencies having waiting areas. You can check this out with the therapist or agency prior to attending therapy for the first time. One strategy people sometimes use is it to locate a therapist outside of the area they live or work in.

If you have any misgivings about therapy, you could reflect on whether the benefits may outweigh your reservations. Reflect on what you would lose or gain by talking to a therapist. Of course, it is up to you if you feel ready to enter therapy; you are free to choose.

International Variation: There is a wide range of views about the stigma of therapy, which will vary across people, families, communities and countries.

Money and time
The question of time, effort and money needing to be spent on therapy to recover and heal is a concern for over 70% of people attending therapy (see Survey Appendix A). After all, you may be just surviving financially or have a

packed life where you don't have the time to add therapy to the list of things you need to do. In this case clearly you can't do therapy. However, I feel it is worth looking closer at the underlying reasons for not entering therapy. The question to ask is, it really about money and time, or are there other factors at play too?

Why would it not be clear whether it's about the money or not? One theory is that money has at least two value factors embedded within it. Money means survival, buying power and opportunities, but it can also represents a relational attachment to money. Because the relationship with money is intrinsic in our lives from childhood, the loss of money or the keeping of money has an underlying "feel" or "thought" process attached to it. The belief may be of "I must not lose money," "I have to save," or even "I will feel down when I spend money," or "I have lost when I lose money." This relationship is built very early in life and reinforced continuously on a daily basis. It is not surprising that our judgements about money and value therefore can be clouded. Having awareness of this I believe can be a useful insight in helping us live the lives we want.

The question you could ask yourself to see if it is really a money issue is to do the following:

- Write down all your expenses and put a value against it (say 1-10).
- What value do you give yourself in healing and growth as a priority against those? Consider the potential future benefits as well as "managing or coping," e.g., better relationships, better mood, or more at peace.
- Are the things you prioritise above yourself related to basic survival, you only, the whole family or to others?
- What specifically would you need to go without to do therapy? Can the priorities below your own priority be forgone, cut out, downsized or put on hold?

You may find going without is easier than having others going without. For example, you may feel guilty that your kids can't go to dance class, go on holiday or it may be that you just want to sustain an accustomed social lifestyle. Really reflect on what it is that you worry about in terms of the financial or time investment.

icking point in people's mind is how you measure the benefits of
when you don't know if it is going to be of benefit, or you don't
ly how "big" that benefit would be. After all, how can you value
when you have not experienced its value? I would recommend
considering the risk and impact to you if you don't get help. For example, the
risk to your wellbeing, quality of life, work, relationships, lost wages, sleep and
time. Even if you do put more value on others, you can see that in fact by
devaluing you, it could still have consequences on you as well as others
regardless. Ultimately, going to therapy can be seen as a sign of valuing
yourself, self-care, compassion and the courage to be open and vulnerable
regardless.

In most cases, you will come to one or more of these conclusions: you really
can't afford therapy, you value yourself less than others, or you could actually
afford it if you cut down in some areas such as your social life, or there are
other factors of concern, such as encounter concerns.

If you conclude you could afford therapy perhaps at a stretch, you can
consider other factors discussed in this book that are reasons for your
reluctance, such as stigma of attending therapy, or performance anxiety. An
oft overlooked factor is that the reluctance to attend could actually be related
to what you are actually trying to overcome such as apathy, hopelessness,
anxiety or being judged. Knowing what blocks you from attending therapy
should be seen as a good sign of progress and an intrinsic part of the healing
process.

Therapy on a budget
One of the most significant challenges society has is providing access to
therapy to those who need it. Therapy has to be paid for somehow regardless
of whether it is free or paid for by the consumer. Unlike the medical model,
service costs for therapy have no guaranteed time limit for when you may get
better. As a solution to reduce costs, a number of approaches are available to
provide cost-effective therapeutic options that are generally short-term based,
for example, solution-focused therapy and CBT is generally applied for the
purposes of overcoming specific problems generally over 1 to 12 sessions.

However, although short-term models of therapy have been hugely beneficial,
it does leave a gap because depending on complexity, severity and how
ingrained the problems are, there are people who would really benefit from a
longer-term approach. The rub is that as per my survey, 70% of people are

very concerned about the financial implications of therapy on their lives. So, the natural question asked is whether there is a lower cost option that can provide the benefits of a longer-term model. Here, I present some ideas for you to consider.

Warning: Please don't take the following ideas as an alternative or equivalent for long-term therapy. They are just ideas that have come about from discussions with others who have had to work on a budget. Seek advice from your physician/doctor and therapist first prior to taking on an alternative route.

- Find a therapist as per the guidance provided in the book that you feel is a right fit for you. You can ask about the possibility of a "sliding scale" fee based on your affordability.
- Use your own reflections and/or a few short-term sessions to identify your problems you are experiencing in detail. You can ask the therapist also what they think you may need to work on. Write down the top 10 underlying difficulties you would want to address. Don't just write addiction or depression; make the difficulties underlying these problems explicit. Examples include jealousy, performance anxiety, anger, finding meaning, boredom, hopelessness.
- Do more reading and education about the problems you have identified through reputable self-help books or online resources. As there are so many to choose from, ask your therapist for any recommendations. Generally, go for books or resources produced by experienced and qualified therapists.
- Use a focused block of sessions to understand how current problems relate to the past. Focus on childhood, family and your upbringing. Try and write a journal or story of your life and how it has affected you. You can return, rewrite and update the narrative of your life as you discover more.
- Read the story and share with any person you trust. They need to be someone who can hear, understand and can keep your personal information private.
- Use several blocks of short term therapy to work on specific related focused issues you have identified above. For example, relational difficulties and anger.

- Supplement short-term therapy with support groups. Many support groups are usually low cost or voluntary and contribution based. You may be able to find support groups that align to your particular issues, e.g., social anxiety, addictions, survivors of abuse. Although these are not therapy groups, they can be used to give and gain feedback, improve communication skills and help you communicate your thoughts and feelings as well as improving relationships.
- If there are particular traumas that have bodily reactions when triggered, plan to work on these longer and consider using trauma-focused therapies such as EMDR.
- Use group therapy. Group therapy are typically lower cost that individual therapy and they give you a chance to explored such as difficulties in forming relationships, patterns of painful relational experiences or addictions.
- Once you have worked through all your underlying issues have a block of sessions to bring together and consolidate what you have learnt into a unified whole that is you.
- Remember, you don't have to work with the same therapist or approach for each block of sessions you use. For example, you could use psychodynamic for talking about childhood impact and existential therapy for looking at purpose in life. In general, I would recommend retaining one therapist who has had the continuous understanding of your therapy process, even if you used several others at different stages.

Further safety considerations

As long as you have a good enough therapist, safety will be an intrinsic part of what you need to feel to enable the work you are doing.

However, you may have existing problems that once triggered, cause difficult emotional or physical reactions, such as a phobia, anxiety or a previous trauma. If you feel you will get triggered emotionally or physically, for example, flashbacks, a phobic reaction, panic, emotional state, fainting, and anxiety, you should let the therapist know beforehand. You can also enquire with the therapist how they intend to keep you safe as possible while working on healing these problems. The therapist should be able to explain how they might mitigate some of the risks through their approach with you.

For example, if you have emotions that triggers when you talk about the trauma the therapist should be able to offer techniques a way of mitigating the difficulties processing memories, such that they don't feel as if you are completely reliving them in the room. Ask the therapist how they intend to keep you safe if you feel you may have these preexisting triggers.

Advice for the concerned

If you are a friend, caregiver, parent or partner of someone who is suffering psychological problems, it is only natural that you may be concerned about their care and want to help them.

In most cases, when you contact a therapist on behalf of someone else, they may vary in how they are able to accept your referral. Generally, if the referral is for an adult, some therapists will insist the adult makes the appointment themselves while for children, it is more acceptable for guardians or parents to refer their child to therapy and thus make appointments on the child's behalf. Either way, the therapist will want to know that the person being referred actually wants to attend therapy for themselves. The reason is twofold: the first, it's unlikely therapy would be helpful for someone who really does not want to enter therapy; secondly, therapy is intended to be safe, and that safety begins from the start with a relationship where information comes from the client. Therapists in general will not want to know your take on an adult client and the issues and problems they have, but rather they want to be informed by the client themselves. However, with children, it is more common to take a few more details.

TIP: Although clients may arrive to therapy "reluctantly" at the beginning, it does not mean that once they begin, they won't change their minds about therapy and its benefits. There is always hope.

It is understandable that you may want to know how things are going for someone you care about in therapy. Some people may wish to talk and some don't and wish to keep information about sessions to themselves. I would advise you to be guided by the person attending therapy and to respect their stance on the matter. However, this does not in most cases mean total disengagement; just show sensitivity to what they are going through and make sure they know they can talk to you if they wish and even that the only reason you don't ask is because you are respecting them. This can be very important given that clients can sometime get the message that people close to them don't care; they perceive no interest as lack of care, which can be especially true for young people. For example, a parent may can be scared of talking about their problems with a child because they believe it will cause them more distress or self-harm.

You may also be worried about the content of what is being talked about in therapy, about you or the family. The therapist is not there to judge you or your family but help them overcome their problems. It is important to give approval to the person receiving therapy they can talk about what they need to. You should bear in mind that good therapists will follow a strict code of ethics included clauses about confidentiality. Confidentiality naturally extends to all relationships outside of the therapist-client relationship, so therapists are unlikely to give you information about how things are going in the therapy process. The only rare exceptions to this would be if there was a serious risk of harm to the client, especially children (see section on Disclosure).

I often get asked by concerned others what they can do for someone who does not want to get help with psychological problems. If they are an adult (18+ in the UK), you cannot do anything unless they are posing an immediate danger to themselves or others. Ultimately you cannot force anyone into therapy or any psychological treatment; it has to be their decision. The best you can do is be patient, offer empathy, provide information and provide possible ways they can get support. Try not to make assumptions and stay calm as possible. If you believe someone may act on suicidal feelings or is at risk of serious harm to self or others, then you should call emergency services.

Further matters of therapist selection

In this section I provide some additional information for consideration when selecting a therapist that have come up in my experience coaching clients' therapeutic process. I look at question about the significance of therapist identification, gender, their age, experience, cost, repeatedly finding the wrong therapist and working with trainee therapists.

Identification matters

Do you prefer a therapist who has a similar background to you? Perhaps the same cultural or national tradition? Or you may prefer someone to have the same stance on spirituality, religious or non-religious? Or even that they have experienced the same problems as you such as abuse, addiction or trauma? There are two views on identification with the therapist.

On one side the therapist who identifies with you may be able to understand your concerns quicker and relate to your life and difficulties. You may perceive they will naturally be on "your side," not judge and understand more of why things have been difficult for you. Having someone who has been through recovery of addiction or child abuse can be beneficial because they have the experience of the process, its struggle, pitfalls and moments of insight.

However, on the other side, there is a school of thought that having a therapist who does not directly identify with you will not come with any preconceived ideas about you because they recognise you for you, with unique experiences that are separate to themselves. So in that sense having someone who has not the same belief or background is thought to be beneficial because they do not hold any fixed view of your world, the outcome or solution.

Remember that the therapist is there to accept you as you are, not to judge, and be beside you all the while being in tune with their own feelings. This does not mean the therapist identifying with you cannot separate themselves from your experience; it is just a theoretical perspective as it depends on the therapist. So I would, unless it is important to you, not dismiss therapists just on the basis of them having a different background because the competence and relational aspects are the foundation of therapy. However, if it is important to you, your beliefs and feeling safe, I would say go with that.

Remember, discounting identity matters in a therapist does not mean you should ignore them having appropriate experience and qualifications for your problems. For example, working with someone who has experience of working with addictions is still important.

Gender matters

I know that it's fairly common for clients to have a gender preference and usually that is based on the client's preference to who they feel comfortable or imagine being comfortable in therapy with. This comfort could be the material to be disclosed which may carry shame or fear that the therapist will judge them. Gender preference could also be more about societal or negative past experiences which become generalised, such as women being more caring and nurturing than men, trust issues, feelings that they would not understand, or be judgmental. Some schools of therapy also believe preferences could be related to past experiences with caregivers and are more subconsciously held, e.g., because of a difficult relationship with their father.

Whatever the reason, you should choose the gender based on who you would feel comfortable with.

However, if you are working on issues you have with a particular gender and you are working through that in therapy, e.g., lack of trust in men, it could be worth considering working with that gender in therapy as it can be used to check out your assumptions and provide new perspectives that ultimately provide a healing experience that maybe needed for your growth. Do what you feel including the feeling that it may be beneficial to work with the opposite gender you normally work with.

Age of the therapist

There is a misconception I feel that age, or grayness, is an important factor in deciding on a therapist because they must know more, be more experienced in years, have more wisdom, knowledge, etc. There may be truth to that but in my experience, this is not necessarily true. Consider that regardless of age, someone could have stagnated their own learning with lacking creativity and focus more on schemas or patterns they have built up over time, may not be as passionate, or importantly not have the life experience you would perhaps imagine someone of that age has. A younger person could in fact have more life experience, be more passionate about therapy, have an openness or be "wise beyond our years." Yes, you need life experience but being younger should not put you off looking deeper and asking the questions I have talked about here. Life experience is certainly an important factor as it in itself can indicate outlook, knowledge and wisdom something that cannot be taught but is more experiential-based. Also remember a younger person being closer in age to your age may be an advantage in terms of similar experience. Age is not necessarily the key, I feel.

Working with the most expensive therapist

Sometimes it is easy to be impressed by a beautiful setting, office building, and letters after a therapist's name, their qualifications and expertise. One therapist may charge £150 an hour and another £35; surely we will be better off with a therapist who charges more? In my experience not really. I would not look at these things as being important, going back to "who they are" rather than "what they are" as being more important and stick with your feelings. Unlike products where you can usually recognise the quality, its function and therefore its value, in therapy that is not always the case. I have been to therapists who charged £35 and ones who charged £80 and the one who charged less I made more progress with; it's not the important factor. Good enough therapists may charge £150 or very little.

Working with Trainee therapists

The short answer is "yes" you can work with trainees as long as they are working within limits. Trainees can have pretty much all the qualities of a good enough therapist; after all, it's the person, right, so it's not in itself an issue. However, my recommendation is that when you are severely distressed or issues that require specialist skills, e.g., with PTSD, you need to be assured emotional safety so in those cases I would not recommend using a trainee. Also, if you are working with a trainee, ask that they are supervised and been given the clear to work with your type of issues. As with any other therapist, only work with them if you're comfortable. It's your therapy and your choice.

Repeatedly finding the wrong therapist

So what happens if you keep going from therapist to therapist and can't find the right one for you? Sometimes it can be that clients don't trust their judgements and make the choices because they themselves dampen down their own real feelings – for example, going along with a therapist you don't really feel comfortable with and saying, "That is just me! I'm going to ignore those feelings." Some other thoughts to consider are that maybe it's not you; it's just that the therapist is not very good, or the way you imagine a good therapist you need is not actually what you really need, or it's just the way it is and there is an incompatibility. Other alternatives are that you just have not found the right one for you yet after all, the process of healing is a journey. When you feel confused about your decisions, I would recommend writing your own journal your own feelings, needs, fears and make it part of the therapeutic journey through self-reflection and have a dialogue with yourself. You can write down an internal dialogue and engage in that to see what is creating the confusion on choice or repeated pattern of going from therapist to therapist, which will help you release and get in touch with your feelings rather than dampen them down. You may also find the self-reflection exercises associated with "finding a therapist" useful to understand what is going on. This type of work also helps you to learn to take responsibility for your own healing. If that does not help, then answering these questions as to why you feel confused, stuck, or overwhelmed by the therapeutic encounter can be really what therapy is about as every client is unique. Take your feelings to the next therapist may lead to unlocking what is going on.

Appendix A – Survey of consumer concerns

The chart below shows the % of respondents in sample of 113 what their concerns were when they first began therapy. By far the most dominant concerns are the therapist being right for the consumer including being competent and non-judgemental, the financial commitment, and personal performance.

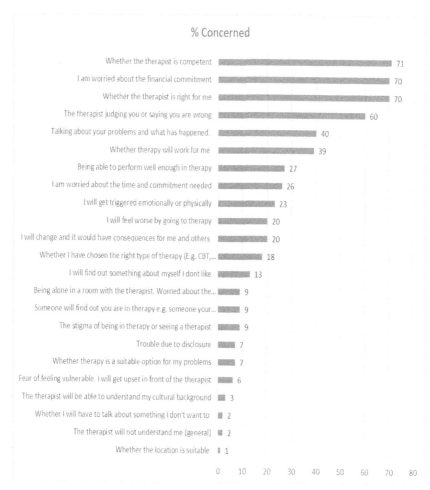

% Concerned

Concern	%
Whether the therapist is competent	71
I am worried about the financial commitment	70
Whether the therapist is right for me	70
The therapist judging you or saying you are wrong	60
Talking about your problems and what has happened.	40
Whether therapy will work for me	39
Being able to perform well enough in therapy	27
I am worried about the time and commitment needed	26
I will get triggered emotionally or physically	23
I will feel worse by going to therapy	20
I will change and it would have consequences for me and others	20
Whether I have chosen the right type of therapy (E.g. CBT,...	18
I will find out something about myself I dont like	13
Being alone in a room with the therapist. Worried about the...	9
Someone will find out you are in therapy e.g. someone your...	9
The stigma of being in therapy or seeing a therapist	9
Trouble due to disclosure	7
Whether therapy is a suitable option for my problems	7
Fear of feeling vulnerable. I will get upset in front of the therapist	6
The therapist will be able to understand my cultural background	3
Whether I will have to talk about something I don't want to	2
The therapist will not understand me (general)	2
Whether the location is suitable	1

Appendix B - Mental health support numbers

If you have seriously harmed yourself – for example, by taking a drug overdose – call your local emergency services or go straight to Accident and Emergency. Or ask someone else to make the call or take you there.

In this section you'll find the international mental health organisations, UK specific mental health support services, reputable UK based counselling and psychotherapy voluntary membership bodies and find a therapist directories.

International mental health organisations

- International Suicide hotline numbers: www.suicide.org, www.befrienders.org
- Worldwide support numbers: togetherweare-strong.tumblr.com/helpline
- Alcoholics Anonymous: http://www.aa.org/
- Narcotics Anonymous: https://www.na.org/
- For people concerned about someone with an Alcohol problem: https://al-anon.org/
- Overeaters anonymous: https://oa.org/worldwide-oa/

UK Based mental health organisations

Childline: 0800 1111
Samaritans: 08457 909090
Abuse Not: 0808 8005015
Brook Young People's Information Service: 0800 0185023
Eating Disorder Support: 01494 793223
Anxiety UK: 0844 477 5774
Depression Alliance: 0845 123 23 20
Rape Crisis Centre: 01708 765200
Rape/sexual assault: 0808 8000 123 (female) or 0808 8000122 (male)
Miscarriage Association: 01924 200799
LLGS Helpline (LGBT): 0300 330 0630
Sexuality support: 01708 765200
Bereavment: 0800 9177 416
Runaway/homeless: 0808 800 70 70
CareConfidential Pregnancy/post abortion: 0800 028 2228
Women's Aid National
Domestic Violence Helpline 0345 023 468
National AIDS Helpline: 0800 567 123

Mental Health Foundation
020 7803 1101
Improving the lives of those with mental health problems or learning difficulties.

Together
020 7780 7300
Supports people through mental health services.

The Centre for Mental Health
020 7827 8300
Working to improve the quality of life for people with mental health problems.

Depression Alliance
0845 123 2320
Provides information and support to those who are affected by depression via publications, supporter services and a network of self-help groups.

PANDAS Foundation
0843 28 98 401 (every day from 9am-8pm)
PANDAS Foundation vision is to support every individual with pre (antenatal), postnatal depression or postnatal psychosis in England, Wales and Scotland. We campaign to raise awareness and remove the stigma. We provide our PANDAS Help Line, Support Groups offer online advice to all and much more.

General advice and support

Young Minds
020 7336 8445
Provides information and advice for anyone with concerns about the mental health of a child or young person.

Childline
0800 1111
Free, national helpline for children and young people in trouble or danger.

Nightline
Listening, support and information service run by students for students.
Other places you could go for support

Age Concern
0800 009966
Infoline on issues relating to older people.

Lesbian and Gay Switchboard
020 7837 7324
Provides information, support and referral services.

Refugee Council
020 7346 6700
The UK's largest organisation working with refugees and asylum seekers.

Relate
0300 100 1234
Offers advice, relationship counselling, sex therapy, workshops, mediation, consultations and support.

Education Support Partnership
08000 562 561
A 24/7 telephone support line which gives teachers access to professional coaches and counsellors 365 days a year. The network also campaigns for change within schools and education policy in order to improve the wellbeing, mental and physical health of teachers.

Anxiety UK
08444 775 774
Works to relieve and support those living with anxiety disorders by providing information, support and understanding via an extensive range of services, including 1:1 therapy.

Generally recognised UK Voluntary Membership bodies
Please note your therapist may belong to another membership body not listed here as there are many others that are equally recognised.

British Association for Counselling and Psychotherapy (BACP)

Address: BACP House, 15, St John's Business Park, Lutterworth LE17 4HB
Telephone: 01455 883300
Email: bacp@bacp.co.uk

UK Council for Psychotherapy (UKCP)

Address: America House, 2 America Square, London EC3N 2LU
Telephone: 020 7014 9955
Email: info@ukcp.org.uk

British Psychoanalytic Council (BPC)
Address: British Psychoanalytic Council, Suite 7, 19-23 Wedmore Street, London N19 4RU
Telephone 020 7561 9240
Email: mail@bpc.org.uk

British Association for Behavioural and Cognitive Psychotherapies (BABCP)
Address: Imperial House, Hornby Street, Bury, Lancashire BL9 5BN
Tel: 0161 705 4304
Email: babcp@babcp.com

Reputable UK directories for finding a therapist
BACP: 01455 883300
Through the British Association for Counselling & Psychotherapy (BACP) you can find out more about counselling services in your area.

Counselling Directory: Counselling-directory.org.uk

UKCP: Psychotherapy.org.uk

Psychologytoday: Psychologytoday.com

Appendix C – Further support

Are you in therapy or are you about to embark on a therapeutic journey? Do you need help? Are you feeling stuck, emotionally overwhelmed, or confused by the healing and growth process of therapy? Do you want to know what direction your healing process should take? Do you need help in figuring out what you need to do to make the process as effective, efficient, and safe as possible? Then these services could be for you.

To support your therapeutic process, I offer the following:

- A secure "Ask the therapist" messaging service
- Online secure coaching (instant messaging, audio, or via web conference)
- YouTube channel "Dear therapist" where you'll find weekly videos from therapists on a wide range of mental health and therapy related matters
- Consumer events (online/offline)

You can find details of each service at empoweringyourtherapy.com.

*These services are for anyone around the world where there are no legal constraints in providing support. It is not for **previous or existing clients for ethical reasons.***

21 Ways to Success in Therapy

Now that you have begun the process you may also want support during the process.

21 Ways to Success in Therapy is a comprehensive (c440 pages) but practical guide for clients to get through therapy successfully, and for therapists to reflect on the struggle clients have in using therapy effectively, efficiently and safely. I put the instrument of therapy (client, process, therapy, and relationship), under the lens of learning theory in coaching clients how they can effect their own change.

Here is the blurb.

21 Ways for Success in Therapy is an in-depth and accessible guide to navigating your therapeutic process in order to be successful within it. By combining how therapeutic change works with what clients do to be successful, this book decodes the most important ways that you can practically apply to effect your change within therapy.

By learning and judging when to apply these ways, you can be confident that you're using therapy effectively, efficiently and safely. These ways can be applied irrespective of type of therapy, your problem, life experiences, symptoms, or even the therapist. If you learn and earnestly apply these ways, you are very likely to be successful.

This book is for both clients and therapists. For clients, this book can be used as a general learning resource to help you get the most from your experience, or as a reference to access when you need help, such as when you're feeling confused, unsafe, overwhelmed or stuck. For therapists, trainee therapists and tutors, this book illuminates the heart of the client struggle to achieve their goals through the instrument of therapy. It can be used as a source of reflection both in the classroom and in practice.

For clients:

- Use therapy effectively, efficiently and safely
- Identify areas you can explore therapeutically
- Overcome obstacles and strengthen your process
- Feel confident in your decisions and the path you're on
- Understand therapy and the process
- Find the right therapist and approach
- Over 70 questions and dilemmas answers
- Demonstration of an end to end therapeutic process

Ask a therapist

If you want to ask me a specific question, you can contact me on the "Ask a therapist" page at empoweringyourtherapy.com.

You can ask questions and they will be answered by a therapist. We will provide some thoughts, reflections, and guidance. The guidance will not be telling you exactly what to do.

Please note that due to legal jurisdiction I may not be able to answer questions if you are based in a particular country.

Online therapy coaching

I also hold confidential online coaching session for clients who need external support for their therapy process. Coaching is based on the principle of working on things that help or hinder you. I do not tell you what to do, but I help to inform your decisions.

The ethics of this services are the same as for psychotherapy and counselling. In particular please note:

- It is confidential unless there is serious harm to yourself or others
- We will provide a safe place for you to share thoughts and feelings from different perspectives and help you to find your own answers
- We will ask questions to help you focus on what's going on but we remain impartial to any decision you make about the direction of your therapy
- We share concerns if something about your process is or maybe harmful to you.

During this process I ask you to fill in a 50 point questionnaire to elicit your feelings and how you are in the room in order to provide some suggested activity to help you with whatever you are struggling with in therapy.

Consumer events

I also hold regular events online and in person for consumers of therapy services. Regular event dates can be found on empoweringyourthearpy.com. Here are the general event details:

This is a psychoeducation event for general public/clients, who are stuck, confused or have overwhelming feelings and emotions that have been created by the therapeutic encounter and process (counselling and/or psychotherapy of any form including individual, couples, group and family therapy).

The types of issues that clients can encounter that could impact their lives include:

- Unsure of direction therapy should take.
- Unsure how to make therapy work for you.
- Don't know whether to stay or leave the therapist.
- How to make therapy efficient, effective and safe.
- Not sure if the therapist is right for you.
- Not sure if you are using the right type of psychotherapy (counselling, CBT, EMDR, DBT etc..) or what options I have.
- Confused feelings towards the therapist.
- Stuck and not making progress.

- Feeling that no therapist is able to help.
- Continuous cycle of starting/ending therapy.
- Finding it hard or ashamed to say things to the therapist you would like to.
- Feeling a loss/attachment towards the therapist even after ending therapy.
- Feeling abandoned by the therapist.
- Feeling angry/frustrated at the therapist.
- Feeling your being blamed by the therapist.
- Feeling the therapist is not being open and/or withholding information.
- Constant thinking about the therapist.
- Emotional and/or therapist abuse, e.g., anger directed towards client.
- Difficult endings in therapy.
- Love and/or sexual attraction.
- Finding it hard to end therapy.
- Detangling feelings between that of a friend and therapist.
- Boundary/ethical issues.

Please note I do not provide a complaints service or a mediation service between the client and therapist or between the client and a professional body.

Contact the author

For questions relating to this book email: ma@paththerapy.co.uk

Appendix D – Eliciting Client Concerns

Clients can begin therapy with questions, concerns, and worries, not only about overcoming their problems or growth but also about therapy, the process, their performance, life impacts, and of course the therapist. Given the range of concerns addressed in this book and described in the questionnaire below, I believe working with these concerns actively has the potential to reduce dropouts, activate client empowerment, align expectations, identify constraints, correct misinformation, identify process interference, tune in your approach, build the relationship, and of course, enable the client's process.

How you wish to work with these questions and concerns will depend on your own approach. There are three approaches, ask direct questions, use an assessment questionnaire or a more client centred approach that naturally falls into talking about concerns.

The Big Questions

Based on the sixty or so concerns that have come up in my research, the following specific questions condense these concerns down into five high-level categories. The following questions do more than simply asking a client "do you have any questions or concerns about therapy?"

- [1] Do you have any questions or concerns about the **suitability** of therapy, the approach or even the therapist to help you achieve your goals?

- [2] Do you have any questions or concerns about yourself, your role and whether you have any worries about being able to "do" therapy? **[personal performance or ability]**

- [3] Do you have any questions or concerns about **safety**, being here with me, saying what you need to say or even about confidentiality?

- [4] Do you have any questions or concerns about therapy **impacting your life**, such as the time commitment or consequences of change?

- [5] Do you have any questions or concerns about how this can help, what will happen or what to **expect** in therapy?

Indirect questions

Questions that can lead to talking more in depth about client concerns include:

- Have you had therapy before? This can lead into discussions about any of the main areas of concerns – Life Impacts, Expectations, Suitability, Personal Ability and Safety.
- Do you have a rough idea of how therapy works? This can lead to discussion about differences between talking in general vs. therapeutic talk, the client role and any concerns
- What expectations do you have about therapy or myself? Or what will work? This can often lead to discussions on expectations, answer concerns and enable work to be tailored to client needs

Inventory of Client Concerns (M-CC)

Apart from achieving your goals in therapy. What are you concerns you most about undertaking therapy? Please remember you are in control, you are not required to answer anything here you are not ready to - just leave any questions blank if that is the case.

Type	Description	Significant Concern	Some Concern
	About you in relation to therapy		
Suitability	Whether therapy is suitable for my problems		
Expectations	What therapy is and what it is not		
Suitability	Whether I will choose the right type of therapy		
Expectations	What I can expect during therapy		
Suitability	Whether I will choose the right therapist		
Expectations	How and why therapy works		
Suitability	How can this help when it's just talking/venting		
Suitability	It will be just like the last therapy e.g. CBT, no direction		
Expectations	What is expected of me in therapy		
Expectations	What will happen in therapy		
	About you in relation to the process		

Type	Description	Significant Concern	Some Concern
Personal Ability	Don't believe I can change		
Personal Ability	Won't feel motivated enough for therapy		
Personal Ability	Unsure whether you are ready to commit or face things		
Personal Ability	Being able to perform to use the sessions to get the most from them		
Personal Ability	I will get triggered emotionally or physically by the experience of therapy (e.g. flashback, phobia, anxiety)		
Personal Ability	I will have to say or answer questions I don't want to		
Personal Ability	Being able to say what I need to say about the problem and what has happens		
Personal Ability	I am fearful of being vulnerable in front of the therapist e.g. being upset in therapy		
Personal Ability	I will feel embarrassed about talking about things that have happened or have experienced in the past		
Personal Ability	I will freeze up and not be able to talk and I'll get blocked		
Personal Ability	Concerned about silences in therapy		
Safety	Confidentiality of sessions (including to spouse, parents)		
	About you in relation to the therapist		
Suitability	The therapist is competent		
Suitability	The therapist has experience with types of problems I am experiencing		

Type	Description	Significant Concern	Some Concern
Suitability	Whether the therapist is the right relational fit for me		
Safety	Therapist will judge, blame me or say I am wrong		
Safety	Being alone in the room with the therapist		
Suitability	They will not understand my race/ethnic background		
Suitability	They will not understand my religious/spiritual beliefs		
Suitability	Whether they can help if they have not been through similar problems or experiences		
Suitability	They will not understand my sexual orientation		
Suitability	They will not understand my lifestyle or behaviors		
Suitability	They won't be able to understand my gender		
Suitability	Therapist won't be able to understand me because of my education, social, or financial status		
Suitability	Whether they will understand me because of age differences (generational)		
Suitability	The therapist is able to meet needs for diagnosis, reports and letters		
	Life Impact to me		
Life Impact	The cost of therapy		
Life Impact	The duration of therapy		
Life Impact	The effort and commitment required of me		
Life Impact	I will feel worse by going to therapy		

Type	Description	Significant Concern	Some Concern
Life Impact	I will change and it will have consequences to myself and others		
Life Impact	I will find something out about myself or others that I don't like		
Life Impact	Someone will find out I am going to therapy		
Life Impact	People will not like that I am in therapy and use it against me e.g. Stigma		
Life Impact	I will or someone will get into trouble if I disclose information to the therapist		
Life Impact	I'll be diagnosed		
	Other		
Safety	What information will be kept and how it will be used (Record Keeping)		
Safety	The impact on an imminent trail (Pre-trial therapy)		
Suitability	Suitability of the location e.g. including for accessibility needs		
Personal Ability	Attending frequency of sessions needed		
Personal Ability	Ability to attend sessions e.g. due to transport, having to care for someone or caring for children.		
Personal Ability	I'll be reliant on medication as a solution		

Mamood Ahmad is a clinical psychotherapist (UKCP Registered) and educator who originated and developed learning centred therapy, a form of therapy and therapy coaching, which focuses on empowering clients to effect their own change within safe and ethical healing relationships, including counselling and psychotherapy.

He has nearly 10 years of therapeutic experience working in private practice with adults, young people, and couples. He is based in Berkshire, UK. He is passionate about family, wing chun (A Chinese martial art), and philosophy.

Learning centred therapy focuses on the client's learning process to effect their desired change against their goals, rather than any specific theory of psychological disturbance.

If you have any comments or questions about the material in this book please send them to: ma@paththerapy.co.uk

If you found this book useful kindly leave a review at amazon books or here .

Reviews are important because it helps to reach people who would find this book useful and in turn support me to continue to write

Printed in Great Britain
by Amazon

87539389R00058